Motor Tr[
Managemcnt

BY

ALAN SHIER
Darlington College of Technology

OXFORD UNIVERSITY PRESS

Oxford University Press, Walton Street, Oxford OX2 6DP

Oxford London Glasgow
New York Toronto Melbourne Auckland
Kuala Lumpur Singapore Hong Kong Tokyo
Delhi Bombay Calcutta Madras Karachi
Nairobi Dar es Salaam Cape Town

and associated companies in
Beirut Berlin Ibadan Mexico City Nicosia

Oxford is a trade mark of Oxford University Press

© Oxford University Press 1977
First published 1977
Reprinted 1983

British Library Cataloguing in Publication Data
Shier, Alan
Motor trade management.
1. Automobile industry and trade — Great Britain —
Management
I. Title
658'.92'920941   HD9710.G72
ISBN 0-19-859150-0

Set by Hope Services, Abingdon
and printed in Great Britain
by J. W. Arrowsmith Ltd., Bristol

PREFACE

This book has been written to follow closely the syllabuses of the Institute of the Motor Industry final examinations (paper 1b Management), the Institute of Road Transport Engineers (section C paper 1 Supervisory Practice), and the City and Guilds Motor Vehicle Technicians Course 390 Part III Principles of Supervision. It has been my experience as Course Tutor on these courses that many students who have followed the normal motor vehicle craft and technician courses find the change from technical study to abstract management theory difficult. I hope that this book will go some way towards overcoming this problem, since it is written in plain English and avoids management jargon. All examples and illustrations are practical and directly related to the motor trade. It is important that readers do not use this text in isolation but make use of the many excellent general management books that are available to broaden their knowledge. I trust that the text will be of value to management trainees contemplating a career in the motor trade; and also to practising managers, in that it may provide an opportunity for them to review their basic management approach. If this is the case then I would like to think it has made some small contribution to improving professionalism in the motor trade.

I would like to acknowledge the help offered by the various motor trade organizations and to thank my friends and colleagues in the trade who often helped me indirectly, and in particular Mr. Watson for his invaluable assistance in checking the final drafts. Finally I am especially grateful to my wife, without whose understanding and encouragement (not to mention her typing and secretarial work) the text would never have reached the publisher.

ACKNOWLEDGEMENTS

Figures 3.9, Ipswich Computer Services Limited; 4.4, R.T.I.T.B.; 5.2, London Brick Company; 5.6, R.T.I.T.B.; 5.7, R.T.I.T.B.; 5.8, R.T.I.T.B.; 5.9, R.T.I.T.B.; 5.10, R.T.I.T.B.; 7.1, S.M.M.T.; 7.2, S.M.M.T.; 7.3, M.A.A.; 7.4, N.J.I.C.; 7.5, R.T.I.T.B.

The author also wishes to thank the administrative staff of the Institute of the Motor Industry, City and Guilds of London Institute, and the Institute of Road Transport Engineers, for their assistance and permission to use past examination questions.

CONTENTS

CHAPTER 1

THE NATURE OF MANAGEMENT

What is a manager's job? Different management writers give varying definitions, based on their own experience or on a particular type of business. For example, if we were to study the work done by a Service Manager, and that done by a Parts Department Manager, the detail of the work involved would be different, but the basic 'management' content would be the same. Certain basic functions are common to all types of manager, whether they manage a garage, a bakery, or an underwear factory; these functions apply in a small private company, a large public company, or even a government department.

A generally accepted method of defining the management function is to use the four elements identified by Henri Fayol, shown in Fig. 1.1.

1. PLANNING. Deciding what shall be done in the future is a very important aspect of management. When a group of people get together to perform a task,

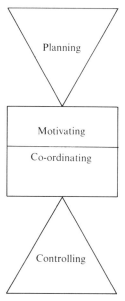

Fig. 1.1   The four basic management functions

someone must decide what operations will be carried out and set objectives. In the motor trade the basic objective will be to offer a service for which customers are willing to pay. In order to do this efficiently a manager must plan the working team and the supply of tools and parts, and set standards of expected performance.

2. CO-ORDINATING. The total work carried out by a garage (or factory) is made up of several different jobs and these must be kept 'in step' or co-ordinated. It is part of the manager's job to keep the operation of different sections within the business, including parts, production, sales, and finance 'in step'. This function takes on more importance as the scope and size of the business increases.

3. MOTIVATING. A very important but often difficult part of a manager's task is to build up the 'morale' or 'team spirit' of the workforce. In many respects a working team is similar to a football team, and the problems of the manager are similar in both cases. A manager dealing with equipment is aware that it will operate in a certain manner, and when dealing with figures knows they can be handled in a logical way. When dealing with people it is not so simple; people tend to act in an irrational manner and their actions cannot always be predicted. To summarize, it is part of the manager's task to get work-people to give of their best.

4. CONTROL. When a manager has made plans, as outlined in (1), his task is not completed, because when plans or goals are set a control system must be used to compare the results achieved with the objectives set. When a deviation from what was expected occurs, the manager must investigate the reasons and take corrective action. For example, if a Service Manager checks a mechanic's booked time against agreed target times, and finds that the time on a particular job is repeatedly excessive, he may well find on investigation that the mechanic requires retraining on that particular job. A similar type of plan-and-control sequence can operate in all departments, particularly in finance.

The control system should be positive and constructive and not the 'big brother is watching you' restrictive type.

Within these four basic elements the manager is also concerned with leadership, decision-making, forecasting, and communication; each of these is dealt with in later chapters. Identifying these functions gives a definition of purpose which is indicative of formal management.

THE DEVELOPMENT OF MANAGEMENT THEORY

Before the industrial revolution formal management and organization existed in the church and in the armed forces. Since industrial production was carried out by small groups of people ('cottage industry') management was informal and there was no necessity to expound theories or commit thoughts to paper. There are isolated examples of both British and American writers producing books on economics, management, and organization from the mid-nineteenth century. At about the turn of this century several manangement writers, particularly in the U.S.A., developed management theories which were labelled 'scientific management'. The following paragraphs give an outline of the life and work of some of the pioneers of management theory. These give a background to the work of the following chapters.

The Pioneers

FREDERICK WINSLOW TAYLOR (1856 – 1915), often called the father of scientific management, was born into a moderately wealthy American family. He had a good education and intended to study law at university, but eye trouble forced him to take up an alternative career. He entered an engineering apprenticeship in 1875, but owing to the industrial depression of the late 1870's he had difficulty finding work in engineering, and so joined the Midvale Steel Works as a production-shop labourer. But Taylor found the workshops in a condition which, in terms of the supply of raw materials, the allocation of work, the work methods employed, and the use made of manpower and facilities, was to his scientific mind appalling. As he gained promotion to gang boss, foreman, and eventually chief engineer, he devoted himself to the task of applying scientific and logical methods of arranging the work to ensure that best use was made of resources, and that workpeople could do a reasonable amount of work in a day. His philosophy was summed up in his own catch-phrase 'a fair day's work for a fair day's pay'.

In addition to his development of scientific management Taylor did research and development on tool steel while working for the Bethlehem Steel Company, from 1890 to 1901. He devoted the remainder of his life to explaining and publicizing 'scientific management' and overcoming ignorance on the part of both managers and workers, who resented his intrusion into what they accepted as normal procedure. This resistance took the form of hostility, sabotage, and personal violence. Although Taylor devoted his life to the application of scientific management and was a very strict disciplinarian, he was also very warm-hearted and human and was sickened by the methods he had to use to get his ideas accepted. When called as a witness before a hostile committee of Congress he explained that his scientific method was not what the average manager or worker considered it to be. 'The great revolution that takes place in the mental attitude of the two parties under scientific management is that both sides take their eyes off the division of the surplus as the all-important matter, and together turn their attention towards the size of the surplus.' 'Both sides must recognize as essential the substitution of exact scientific investigation and knowledge for the old individual judgement or opinion, either of the workmen or boss, in all matters relating to the work done in the establishment'.

FRANK BUNKER GILBRETH (1868 – 1924), was also an American, with a good educational background. He was educated at Boston Grammar School and qualified to enter Massachusetts Institute of Technology, but decided to enter the building industry and became a bricklayer's apprentice. He attended evening classes and worked in various different trades in the construction industry, and at the age of 27 he was appointed Chief Superintendent (Managing Director) of the company.

In the early weeks of his apprenticeship he noticed that each bricklayer used his own individual method when doing his work, and thought that surely *one* method must be more efficient than all the others.

In 1895 Gilbreth set up his own contracting business in Boston and did pioneer work in what is now known as pre-stressed concrete. The business expanded very rapidly over a large part of the U.S.A., and also to London.

During this time Gilbreth published several books on building methods and techniques, each concentrating more and more on method. With the increasing interest in method study and the psychological aspects of management he decided to become a management consultant, assisted by his wife Lilian, who was a trained teacher and took a keen interest in psychology. Development of motion study was very rapid during the First World War, when Gilbreth acted as a consultant in both the U.S.A. and Europe.

Motion study as used today is based on the work of the Gilbreths. It involves a close observation of the separate operations involved in a job, careful analysis of these operations, and re-arrangement of the operations to form a new, more efficient method. The results of work study in Gilbreth's own company were that a bricklayer's output was increased from 1000 bricks per shift to 2700 bricks per shift.

A social group was formed by people working in the movement toward scientific management; and through this group Gilbreth was in contact with Taylor and Gantt.

The Gilbreths' work in motion study was summed up in their catch phrase 'one best way'.

HENRY LAURENCE GANTT (1861 – 1919) gave his name to a bar chart (see Fig. 4.5) which is particularly useful in planning. It is unfortunate that other very important aspects of his work are often forgotten. Gantt was interested in scientific management from the point of view of the worker and was an originator of the term 'industrial democracy'. He was born of a wealthy family of Maryland farmers, but the family fortune was lost in the Civil War. He attended the McDonagh School, where he received a very practical education from the age of 12 to 17. He then attended university and after qualifying returned to the McDonagh Institute as a mathematics and science lecturer, and later as a practical instructor. Gantt's career was similar to that of both Taylor and Gilbreth in that he had two roles, that of a technician and executive in industry, and that of a consultant and management thinker. On leaving his teaching career he joined the staff of the Midvale Steel Works and in 1888 was appointed assistant to the Chief Engineer, F.W. Taylor. His main duties in this post involved 'determining the most economical methods of working the machine tools in the machine shops'. He was then promoted to superintendent of the casting shop. He left Midvale in 1893 and held executive posts in several different enterprises. January 1901 saw the formation of Gantt Management Consultants. Up to his sudden death in 1919 he covered fifty assignments, each of which he supervised personally. These included detailed work for many leading American firms, covering working methods, work systems, bonus schemes, and training schemes. Gantt would only work for clients who were sympathetic to his theories. He himself stated 'before I undertake to do any work for any concern, I ask the people employing me, or who contemplate employing me, to read this little book, *Work, Wages, and Profits*. I ask those people who have in mind employing me whether they are in accord with the ideas expressed in the book, of how to handle their workmen and what share the workmen will have in what is being done. Unless they are willing to subscribe substantially to what I have written in the book, I have always declined to do any work for them.' This shows that, like Taylor, he required a complete change in management's attitude; and also shows his preoccupation with the human aspect of management. He wrote: 'the idea of setting for each a task with a bonus for its accomplishment seems to be in accord with human nature, and is hence the proper foundation of a system of management.'

HENRI FAYOL (1841 – 1925) was of French nationality and graduated from university as a mining engineer at 19 years of age. He took up the post of technician in a colliery; but quickly rose to become manager of the colliery group by 1869. Later more collieries were added; but the whole combine of which Fayol's group was part began to fail financially, and was verging on bankruptcy. Since Fayol's Commentry – Fourchambault group had been successful he was asked to become General Manager of the whole combine when he was 47. When he retired in 1918 he left a very large combine, which was financially stable and expanding its assets.

Fayol's famous book *Administration Industrielle et Générale* (General and industrial administration), published in 1916, lists five elements in the basic management process: (a) planning (b) organizing (c) motivating (d) command (e) control. Modern definitions do not list 'command' as a separate item, but include it under 'control' and 'motivation'. Fayol probably placed emphasis on command because he was involved in such a large, diverse, and scattered enterprise. He dealt particularly with the improvement of administration. Although Fayol's work was part and parcel of the scientific management movement, and there are parallels between him and both Taylor and Gilbreth (e.g. practical training followed by a move to management), he worked from the top of the organization downwards. He explained that his principles applied to government departments and other organizations as well as businesses. He did not envisage administration as a function set apart or set above others, but as a special function requiring special training and management skills. His book also lists fourteen administrative principles and sixteen everyday administrative rules.

MARY PARKER FOLLETT (1865 – 1933) differs from other pioneers in that she had no direct connection with industry. She was a student of philosophy and psychology at Harvard and Cambridge. She studied the psychological reactions of individuals and groups of people. Unlike other pioneers she was not directly concerned with methods, systems, and control, but she was interested in studying basic human emotions and the emotional forces that come into action when people are grouped, and groups formed into organizational structures. Unlike Fayol she looked at the problems of the individual worker, and studied the organization upwards from there.

In 1900 she opened the Roxbury Neighbourhood House in Boston which provided recreational, social, and educational facilities for boys and girls from the poor area of the town, who worked long hours in factories and workshops. This single venture developed rapidly, and the movement to provide similar facilities became nationwide. Mary Follett was appointed Chairwoman of the Committee on the extended use of school buildings in 1909.

The next logical development was the provision of vocational guidance centres. She also served on committees dealing with wages. In her later years she became famous as a great writer and thinker. She advocated that the employee/employer relationship should be one of co-operation, rather than one of a superior passing orders to subordinates. Like Taylor she pleaded for a new outlook on industry, but went further, saying that it should be placed in perspective as one part of the organized life of the community.

ELTON GEORGE MAYO (1880 – 1949) was born of a middle-class Australian family. He attended St. Peter's College, Adelaide and later Adelaide University, where he took a degree in philosophy. After graduating he moved to Edinburgh where he studied the psychological aspects of medicine. He continued his interest in psychology when he treated shell-shocked soldiers in Australia during the First World War. Following the cessation of hostilities he accepted the Chair of Philosophy at Queensland University. Later he was attracted to the U.S.A. to do more research. He moved to Pennsylvania in 1923 and studied physical fatigue among textile workers; and to Harvard University School of Business Administration in 1926. His work had led him to develop some basic theories on the importance of small groups in industry in relation to productivity. While he was at Harvard he was asked to lead a research team investigating the effects of light intensity on the work at the Hawthorne Plant of the Western Electric Company.

The Hawthorne Investigation (1924 – 1927), as this research later became known, began as a simple series of tests on the effects of illumination on output, but developed into a more far-reaching and fundamental study. The initial tests were carried out with two groups of workers assembling electrical units. One group worked under normal conditions, while the second worked under conditions where the light intensity could be varied. The totally unexpected result that emerged was that production rose over-all in both groups; and the test group increased productivity when the researchers told them that the illumination would be increased, but in fact it was not. This result led Mayo to conclude that the main factors affecting productivity were psychological rather than physical. This led to the initiation of the 'Hawthorne Investigations' proper, which progressed in three stages, each developing from the previous one.

(1) *The Relay Room Tests* involved small groups of workers assembling telephone relay units. Working conditions were varied by changing working hours; the length of the working week; rest periods; rates of pay; and the temperature and humidity of the work-place. It was found that no matter how physical working conditions were changed, productivity afterwards remained 25 per cent higher when conditions were back to normal. These results reinforced the finding of the original study, and led to a second stage involving the entire workforce.

(2) *Interview studies.* This stage of the study used a mass interview technique involving 21 000 workers. The basic idea was to determine objectively the features of the working environment which the workers liked and disliked, and from the results make arrangements that would enhance job satisfaction. In practice it was found difficult to assess with any accuracy the true reasons for an individual's dissatisfaction. These problems led to specialized and sensitive interviewing techniques and skills, which brought about an off-shoot of the main objectives; individual employees gained a better understanding of their general and working environment and their personal conflicts. This interviewing technique has since been developed extensively and forms the basis of 'personnel

counselling'. The main study results indicated that dissatisfactions were based on the person's total environment and past experience, factors which could not readily be rectified by physical working conditions.

(3) *The Bank Wiring Observations*. This study was limited to groups of fourteen men and their supervisors. It differed from the relay room tests in that the group worked under normal conditions and no artificial physical working conditions were applied. The methods used a combination of interviews and observations of the group, reflecting Mayo's earlier studies in Australia. The findings showed that the working group was a complex organization in itself. It established its own structure and set its own goals, which were not necessarily related to those officially laid down. They also showed that separate members of the group lost their individuality in order to conform to the standards of the group.

The results of these investigations allowed the Western Electric Company to take a lead in developing modern industrial relations; and Elton Mayo as leader of the investigations has since been recognized as a pioneer in this field.

B. SEEBOHM ROWNTREE (1871 – 1954) brings the development of management theory nearer to home and closer to our time. Seebohm was born into a wealthy York family. He was educated at the Friends' School, York, and at Owen's College, Manchester, where his studies included social research. After returning to the family business at York he was made Labour Director, and took a great interest in improving conditions for the workers. He realized that workpeople could not give of their best if they were concerned about their future, so he pioneered pension schemes.

The 1914–18 war saw a very rapid expansion of munition production, without any provision of welfare facilities. Rowntree was appointed Head of the Industrial Welfare Department. While serving in this government post he established the foundation of modern welfare methods; and he also carefully observed many examples of inefficient and ineffective management. He travelled to the U.S.A. annually from 1921 to 1939 to study and keep in touch with the progress of scientific management. From 1923 onwards the Cocoa works at York were a splendid example of advanced industrial relations where workers' fears were as far as possible removed. He organized courses of further education and re-training within the firm. He introduced unemployment pay, canteens, recreation facilities, and company housing. At York all rules were made by a committee; a shop steward elected by the trade unions but paid by the firm was employed full-time to sort out workers' problems; and workers were kept in touch by a 30-man elected committee and an annual 'open meeting'. Rowntree stressed that the cost of these worker benefits had to be met by improved management.

Although showing great interest in human relations and industrial democracy, he was a shrewd businessman and an energetic manager whose enthusiasm 'filtered down' through the whole organization.

Space does not permit a full coverage of all pioneers but students should endeavour to study the work of other writers, up to and including present-day authors such as Col. Urwick, E.F.L. Breck, J. Munro Fraser, and Peter Drucker (see Recommended Reading List).

MANAGEMENT: AN ART OR A SCIENCE?

Much has been written expounding the theories that 'management is an art' or that management is a science, but the volume of this has tended to decrease during the last 20 years, since the argument has been tempered with common sense. An appreciation of these two opposed views is useful in that it does prompt us to consider in detail the qualities we require in an effective manager.

Management as a science. Devotees of this argument state that the main task of a manager is to collect facts and figures on a particular situation, apply some form of evaluation to these and, from this, reach a conclusion. The most effective way this can be done is by using a scientific approach such as would be used by a chemist or a physicist. This will give the most effective results, and will lead to the formation of a set of principles which will build up into a framework, to give a good control system and an effective workforce.

Management as an art. Proponents of this argument see the major part of the manager's task as that of leadership. Therefore a good manager must possess qualities of leadership, which he would have as part of his personality and character. Since personality has many facets, certain qualities spring to mind such as enthusiasm, sincerity, confidence, and magnetism, which form part of this personal phenomenon of leadership.

With a little thought it is obvious that either of these theories cannot be treated as a separate entity. If such a person as the theoretically ideal manager existed he would possess both the quality of leadership and the ability to apply a scientific type of analysis to his work. Few managers can possess all the required qualities, but an efficient manager will use his personal atttributes (leadership) with his professional education and training. Therefore we can summarize very briefly by saying that both innate and acquired qualities are required in an effective manager.

MANAGEMENT'S RESPONSIBILITIES TO FOUR SOCIAL GROUPS

The essential purposes of a business are to make a profit and to provide goods or services. If a dealership is to do this successfully it must also fulfil certain social responsibilities, which for convenience can be divided into four groups.

The customer. The dealer aims to provide the service or products the customer requires at an acceptable quality and reasonable cost, and generally to look after the customer's interests. It has been stated that 'the customer is the true employer of labour', in that if the customer does not require the service offered there is no necessity for the enterprise to exist. Every employee and manager must understand and appreciate the importance of the customer. It is particularly important in such areas as vehicle sales and service reception, but it must be appreciated by all employees, most of whom do not meet the customer face to face.

The employees. Most employees could draw up a list of factors which affect their job satisfaction. In broad terms these are: security of employment, fair financial rewards for work done, good working conditions, etc.

The shareholders have invested capital to finance the activities of the firm; and they expect a reasonable return on this captial. In addition to this, the business must be run in such a way as to ensure the future security of the money invested.

The locality. Any business, large or small, has some effect on the locality in which it is situated. In the case of large manufacturing industries this can involve atmospheric pollution, disposal of waste, etc. In the case of a garage the effect is on a smaller scale, and could involve connections to services, movement of vehicles, the dispersion of fumes, and noise.

It is of benefit to both the company and the locality to develop a public conscience, as many forward-thinking firms purposely do, and become involved in social activities, the arts, and special local events. The four conflicting interests described above are shown diagrammatically in Fig. 1.2.

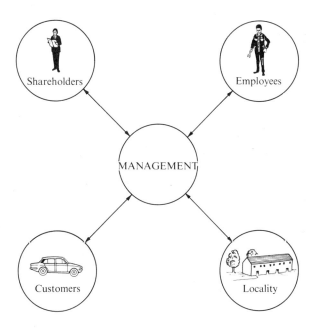

Fig. 1.2   Management's responsibilities to the four social groups

These responsibilities are responsibilities of the business as a whole, and are therefore the responsibility of top management. From the manager's standpoint all four groups are important, because in practice he must strike a compromise between the interests of each of these groups, which may be in competition: e.g. if a workshop improved its methods and greatly increased its profit, this increase could be used to further the interest of either the shareholders, customers, employees, or the locality.

POLICY

A phrase used glibly by managers is 'it is our policy to . . .'; and in some cases the manager will use the word 'policy' without really know what policy is. If a manager is to perform the four functions listed above he must have a known purpose, and a set of guide-lines within which he can work. The responsibility for the formulation of policy lies with the governing body of the organization. In the motor trade this is usually the proprietor or the board of directors. The formulation of good general policy should be a deliberate act on their part, although it can be based on procedure established in the past or some established procedure and recommendations from supervisors and managers.

The general policy should

(a)   state the aims and purpose of the company,

(b)   be applicable to all departments and sections,

(c)   cover all foreseeable conditions,

(d)   form a general set of rules to be followed in recurrent situations,

(e)   take into account all relevant laws and regulations,

(f)   be worded in such a way as to allow managers to use their initiative and make their own decisions within the policy.

This general policy covers the whole company, which can then be subdivided by either function (e.g. sales, finance, personnel) or by departments (e.g. workshop, sales, parts, etc.) and a policy lying within the general policy drawn up by each manager for his own department.

Having drawn up a good general policy and departmental policy, these must then be communicated to everyone involved in the company. This can be done by word of mouth, via managers, supervisors, foremen, charge hands, etc.; but this tends to be unreliable and the message is often distorted. A much better method is for the policy to be in a written form (e.g. typed pages in a ring binder). It should be worded in such a way as to be easily understood by the person concerned. This may require different 'translations' for different levels in the organization.

The final step in a meaningful use of policy is that managers have a responsibility to ensure that all operations and activities are being carried out within the guide-lines of policy.

DECISION-MAKING

All aspects of the operation of a dealership involve decisions of one sort or another. Decision-making forms the basis of all management action. The job of managing in its truest sense consists largely of planning and decision-making. The American management writer Peter Drucker has identified management decisions as 'tactical' — those which are the less important, routine decisions; and 'strategic' — decisions involving the collection of facts and figures with a view to making decisions that are long-term, or will affect the policy or working methods of the dealership or department. The levels of decision-making in organization structures can be classified as:

(i)   corporate decisions: the responsibility of the managing director and board of directors or proprietors, involving long-term objectives, general policies, and the future of the firm.

(ii) operational decisions: the responsibility of the managers of each department (e.g. service manager, parts manager). These relate to the day-to-day, month-to-month operation of the department within the corporate plans.

(iii) supervisory decisions: taken in the place of work on a day-to-day basis and lying within a supervisor's defined area of responsibility.

An effective manager must see himself as a specialist in making decisions, and must develop a philosophy of objective decision-making based on fact. The complexity and nature of modern business is such that the old image of the general manager making snap decisions based on initiative and instinct has given way to rational decision-making based on analysis of the facts concerned. The environment of the decision-maker will obviously have some bearing on the decisions made; but every effort must be made to deal with facts in an unbiased manner, avoiding personal preferences and beliefs, and ensuring a clear-cut approach. Basically the task of the decision-maker is to select from a number of alternatives a course of action which will give the desired result and achieve a certain objective.

There is some confusion among management writers in defining 'decision-making' and 'problem-solving'. This confusion can be avoided by considering decision-making as part of the planning process and therefore forward-looking; while problem-solving is necessary when events occur in the running of a business which are outside what was planned. Once one has accepted these basic definitions the logical framework shown below, which can be applied to either situation, can be used.

1. Define the problem. The manager must make a diagnosis of the situation, since what is brought to his attention is a symptom and requires him to find the root cause. An analogy can be drawn with a visit to the family doctor: the patient explains the symptoms from which he is suffering, and the doctor must then diagnose the true cause of the symptom. It is important that adequate time is devoted to this stage, allowing a full investigation. In all probability a quick answer will be the wrong one.

2. Listing alternatives. Having isolated the root cause of the problem, the next step is to draw up as many alternative solutions as possible. At this stage practical limitations need not be considered, the object being to draw up a comprehensive list, including alternatives which may appear at first glance to be extreme or 'way out'. If restrictions on the alternatives are imposed at this stage innovation and initiative may be stifled; and a manager may tend to concentrate on a limited range of alternatives. A factor often taken into account by progressive companies in management-appraisal schemes is originality and innovation in management thinking. Effectiveness at this stage can be improved by involving subordinates where possible. This gives the advantages of group judgement and synthesis of opinions, without the formation of a committee, since information can be collected orally or by memoranda.

3. Comparing alternatives. The list drawn up at stage 2 must now be analysed and a list of pros and cons drawn up for each alternative. Limiting factors will eliminate alternatives which could not possibly be put into practice. Factors which must be taken into account are: the effect of the decision on employees and customers; its effect on productivity and profit; its time span; its effects on other departments; and whether the decision is unique or is likely to recur. If decisions are likely to recur a record of facts and figures should be made which will save managerial time in the future. The result of this comparison is a short-list of alternatives.

4. Selecting the solution. From the short-list the course of action which will achieve the desired results is selected. The choice is usually a compromise, being the one that will give the best results with the minimum of cost and disruption. The theoretically best solution is often only marginally better than one which is more easily available.

5. Implementing the decision. A decision can only become effective when action is taken, although it must be borne in mind that taking no action is just as much a decision as making a major change. Since most business decisions involve people, communication is vital at this stage. Therefore, as well as making the physical changes such as re-arranging workshop layout, changing office procedure, or revising the accounts system, the human aspect must play a major role. Since people tend to prefer the *status quo*, those involved in implementing the decision must understand the reason *why* changes are to be made, as well as *what* is expected of them and their colleagues.

6. Evaluate results. Just as a control system is necessary when implementing plans, so it is necessary to evaluate the results of a decision when it is put into action. Even a poor decision can perhaps be salvaged by being modified; or, if not, its failure can be noted for use when making decisions in the future.

The above six steps provide a grid or framework on which decision-making or problem-solving can be based. In practice a manager will not proceed in the decision-making process in six isolated steps; they would form a continuous process. By using a sequence like this, a manager is more likely to make effective decisions consistently. This type of analysis can be effective using only pen and paper; but in cases where decisions will be far-reaching, or where a large quantity of data is being analysed, mathematical methods, such as Operational Research, which has been in use since the early 1950s, can be used. In this technique variables such as work loadings, the use of equipment and customer patterns are analysed (using a computer to process the data), and the optimum amount of personnel and equipment to give cost-effective operation is calculated. These techniques have the advantage that changes can be made and the end result tested on the computer before a final decision is made. These new techniques are tools of management, which present the manager with information and possible alternatives. The decision and responsibility for the decision must still rest with the manager.

EFFECTIVE USE OF EXECUTIVE TIME

The Managing Director's, and General Manager's, and indeed other managers' jobs, need to be systematically organized. The greater the manager's responsibilities, the more important it is that he makes the best use of his time. At higher levels a manager tends more and more to 'take his work home', not necessarily in the physical sense that he takes a brief-case full of papers home, but in the sense that he finds it more difficult to 'switch off' as he leaves work, and continues to carry on working mentally.

If a manager is to make the best use of his time it is necessary to study his job, much as work-study is applied to a mechanic on the shop floor. This systematic study can be carried out in three stages ('the three Rs').

(i) *Record:* In work-study the initial step is to record what is happening at the present time. The manager must draw up a timetable for a typical week's work. To gain a true picture it must be an average week, typical of his usual work-load. If the area of work is variable it may be necessary to record over a longer period of time. The timetable can be based on 10- to 15-minute intervals, much like a school timetable; or time expenditure on various tasks can be recorded by noting the time they begin and end. This step in itself encourages the manager to be a 'clock watcher', and become more aware of time.

(ii) *Review:* When completed, the timetable should be reviewed and analysed. This can be done by drawing up a Time Analysis Chart under a series of headings to show the main categories of work, such as: contacts with superior; contacts with subordinates; analysing performance; planning; and personal problems of staff. Each of the activities, and the time it takes, can then be classified under these headings, with work which does not readily fit into any category being entered under 'miscellaneous'. When the chart is completed the analysis can be carried out by critically but constructively answering such questions as:

Are the category headings what they should be for the particular management post?
Is the time balance between them correct?
Is sufficient time being spent on communication with superiors and subordinates?
Is time being spent on tasks which are not true management tasks and should be delegated?
Is time allowed for the personnel/human aspects?
Is a large percentage of time lost on miscellaneous items?

(iii) *Re-organize:* Answers to questions such as those above lead to a re-organizing of the time outlay and work schedule. The revised schedule is probably more effective if it is written down, at least at this stage. Tasks should be placed in subject groups, so that similar jobs are carried out at the same time. Timing should be arranged to give realistic blocks of time, with a minimum of interruptions. Routine and recurring tasks could be delegated after an initial decision has been made. Finally, a careful scrutiny of items classified as 'miscellaneous' should be made, since it is in this area that time can be wasted in the true sense of the word. This is often due to the fact that changes in the organization or changes in methods of working have made a work-schedule that was once effective, out of date. In addition to this, people tend to work in a routine which they develop over a period of time; once established they are reluctant to change this pattern, because it has become a habit. From this analysis, a revised timetable can be drawn up and the time saved put to effective use. It is a natural human inclination unconsciously to fritter away time that has been saved, and this must be avoided, or else the whole object of the analysis is lost. This type of analysis has been criticized as a 'paper exercise' unrelated to reality. This criticism is only valid if the manager sees his revised timetable as one he must slavishly follow. The 'recording' and 'reviewing' are probably the most important stages, since they will have made him more aware of his management role, and his use or misuse of time. The re-organized timetable can then be used as a flexible guide towards the maximum effective utilization of his time. This in turn will need to be revised as the dealership develops.

QUESTIONS

1. Discuss how the work carried out by Taylor and Gilbreth contributes to the efficient management of a modern garage. (I.M.I.)
2. Describe the work of any one management pioneer and show how his contribution has influenced modern management practice. (I.M.I.)
3. Describe the contribution made to the development of management thinking by any one of the following:

Henri Fayol
Mary Parker Follet
Elton Mayo   (I.M.I.)

4. Give some examples of the way in which a management's business objectives can conflict with its responsibilities to society. Suggest how such conflict may be resolved. (I.M.I.)
5. What steps can a manager take to ensure that he has time to deal effectively with important matters? (I.M.I.)
6. Describe the nature of decision-making. What steps would you suggest to improve decision-making in an organization? (I.M.I.)
7. 'Decision-making is an essential function of every manager.' Outline the basic principles of good decision-making and describe some common errors.
(M.A.A./I.M.I.)

CHAPTER 2

ORGANIZATION

Any dealership is made up of individuals or groups of workers and supervisors, who perform different jobs (e.g. foremen, mechanics, salesmen, partsmen) in order that the dealership can achieve its objective of offering services to the public.

Organization is the *framework* which brings the activities necessary to achieve the objectives of the dealership and the facilities necessary for the performance of those activities into efficient working relation to one another.

Fayol recognized that muddling along with an ineffective structure would lead to chaos. Quite often organizations in the motor trade have evolved over a period of time, without any real thought being given to the organizational structure.

Although the bulk of businesses in the motor trade are of small to medium size, with many partnerships and one-man businesses, the current tendency is towards the formation of large dealerships and groups. It is unlikely that a reader will have the opportunity to plan an organization from scratch, but it is quite possible that a person attaining a management post in a large dealership will have to re-build or re-plan an existing structure which is ineffective or out of date. The basic stages involved in planning a structure are ('the Six Ds'):

1. *Decide* the basic functions involved: e.g. repairs, body repairs, parts department;
2. *Divide* these functions into sections and groups: e.g. parts department, service department, vehicle sales;
3. *Determine* the relationship between the various groups;
4. *Devise* a formal system of communication throughout the organization;
5. *Design* a suitable system of control;
6. *Depict* the completed structure in the form of a chart.

ORGANIZATION CHARTS

Organization charts usually show:

The Managing Director, General Manager, or Chief Executive;

Departmental Managers;

Lines of authority and responsibility;

Official titles of other personnel (and possibly names).

Basic Types of Organization Structure

LINE. This occurs where a senior post carries greater responsibility and authority than the post immediately below it in the line of authority. For example a Service Manager is in a line position in relation to a General Manager, and the Workshop Foreman to a Service Manager. In this type of structure the 'lines of authority' can clearly be seen running from the top to the bottom of the chart, so forming a single 'chain of command'.

The main advantage of this type of structure, shown in Figs 2.1 and 2.2, is that lines of communication are short and direct (often with face-to-face contact between the people concerned) and problems can be solved and decisions reached quickly. Also the customers have direct contact with the people concerned, thus creating a more personal relationship. The main disadvantage is that as the size of the business increases the structure eventually becomes inadequate and overloads the Proprietor.

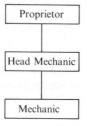

Fig. 2.1   Simplest form of line organization

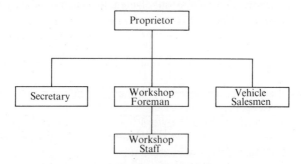

Fig. 2.2   Line organization typical of a small garage
(These types of organization structure are so simple that charts would not be drawn in practice.)

LINE AND STAFF. If the business shown in Fig. 2.2 expands and becomes more diversified, the increasing volume of work will mean that at some time the Owner/Manager will not be able to handle all his duties personally, and at this point *one* possible modification to the structure is to create a *staff position*, which in this case would be that of Assistant to the Manager (Fig. 2.3).

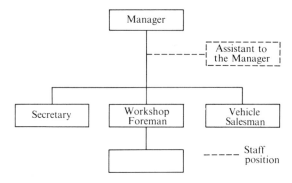

Fig. 2.3   Line and staff

A staff position is not in the direct line of authority, and therefore does not carry the responsibility or authority of a line position. The Manager does not delegate authority; the staff handles routine everyday tasks and generally assists the manager, while the manager retains the right of decision-making and authority, so that the staff becomes an extension of the Manager's working capacity.

FUNCTIONAL. This type of organization originated with F.W. Taylor's 'functional foremanship', and has been the centre of a terminological tangle since the 1920s. However it is generally accepted that functional relationships occur in any organization where a specialist executive or manager, such as a personnel manager, exercises only an indirect authority over members of other departments, since he always goes through the respective line managers, as in Fig. 2.4. As soon as the manager of a small garage decides to avail himself of the services of an accountant he has subdivided his management duties, and a 'functional' relationship has been formed.

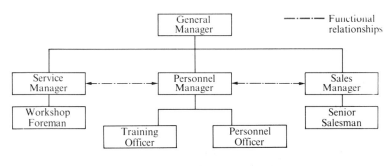

Fig. 2.4   Functional

Using this definition a functional organization cannot exist as an individual structure without line positions, and structures used in practice combine line, staff, and functional types of organization (Fig. 2.5). A manager should not

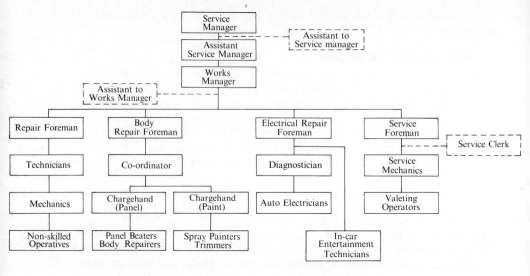

Fig. 2.5   Organization of a large service department

place too much importance on labelling types of structure. What is required is a combination of those types that will be most effective in operation. Organizational planning should be based on responsibilities and relationships and the logical grouping of these.

Advantages of Organization Charts.

1. The fact that a chart has been drawn means that detailed study of the structure must have been made.
2. Relationships between departments and sections are shown.
3. Responsibilities at each level can be clearly defined.
4. The chart showing the existing structure forms a good basis for modifications and alterations.
5. Charts form a useful ready reference for a person from outside the organization or for the essential induction of new members of staff.

Disadvantages.

1. The chart can quickly become out of date as the structure changes as a result of economic pressures, staffing changes, and expansion.
2. Because the chart shows very rigid lines of communication and authority it can lead to painfully slow communications and decision-making, if the lines are strictly followed; in practice short cuts are taken.
3. The lines show a static structure; but the organization is made up of people and the chart cannot show changing and complex human relationships.
4. Staff may tend to stick rigidly to their specified responsibilities, and this results in a lack of flexibility.

Although organization charts have inherent disadvantages, they perform a very useful function in any organization. Charts should be drafted by a person who is familiar with them. They should be kept up to date by a half-yearly or annual review.

UNOFFICIAL ORGANIZATION

An organization chart portrays the formal relationships and main channels of communication. This can be drawn up before people are 'placed in little boxes'. At this stage the structure is static. When the organization becomes operational a pattern of relationships develops between all the persons involved in the structure and connected with it. If it were possible to show all these complex relationships on a chart it would show a configuration differing from that of the organization chart. In practice these relationships are superimposed on the official structure, and the actual channels of communication may be completely different from the official channels, since information may flow downward and across the organization through informal channels. For example, on the chart shown in Fig. 2.5 a relationship may exist between the Assistant Service Manager and a cleaner, in that they meet and chat at break times. If the Assistant Service Manager passes some information to the cleaner, the cleaner may pass the information to the semi-skilled operator, or to the mechanics, shop foreman, etc. The information will then be flowing in exactly the opposite direction to that of the official line of communication in that department. A Manager must be aware that these social relationships exist, and are important in the everyday activities of the dealership.

An interesting recent development in the management structure of motor-trade dealerships has been the establishment of hierarchies based on basic management functions rather than on the traditional skills of sales, service, and parts. In the new structure duties are arranged under marketing, technical, and business managers, who deal with these basic functions in all departments. The basic idea is to improve management.

It is important that all staff forming the organization are trained in their respective jobs to R.T.I.T.B. standards. This applies as much to supervisors and managers as to other staff. This will enable the dealership to operate as smoothly as possible.

DELEGATION OF RESPONSIBILITY AND AUTHORITY

The act of delegation takes place when a superior entrusts certain operations, or part of the dealership's work, to a subordinate, and the subordinate accepts the obligation. It does not mean a surrender of responsibility by the superior. In simple terms the subordinate is responsible for doing the job and the superior for ensuring that the job is done.

As a dealership expands, we have seen that staff positions, and later functional departments, can be formed. At each stage the Owner/Manager is delegating different responsibilities. This process is then repeated at all levels in the organization. If delegation is to be effective the subordinate must:

  (a) understand and accept the responsibility assigned to him,
  (b) understand and accept how the end result will be measured,
  (c) be given authority comparable to the responsibility, and
  (d) be held responsible by checking his actual performance against agreed realistic goals or objectives.

Let us assume that the Service Manager delegates *responsibility* for workshop loading to a Workshop Controller. The Controller's performance can be evaluated by the percentage of worktime during which the workshop is fully loaded, rather than only partially loaded, but with a large number of vehicles still left awaiting repair. The Workshop Controller must have complete *authority* over the arrangements for jobs in the workshop and the necessary staff. If the Service Manager finds that this aspect of the Controller's work is below standard, he must deal with this by explaining to the Controller that his performance is not satisfactory. It would be a mistake to issue conflicting orders about workshop loading, for this would reduce the authority and responsibility of the Controller. Delegation will only be effective if managers define clearly where the responsibility for each worker and supervisor begins and ends. And this implies an equally clearly defined division of authority among the managers themselves; for the responsibilities delegated must be matched by parallel authority. Although the organization chart is useful in giving a pictorial view of the relationships, more details of responsibilities can be included in a 'responsibility schedule', an example of which is shown in Fig. 2.6. These schedules are used in conjunction with the organization chart to give full details of responsibilities and authority in the dealership, and they can form the basis of an organization and policy manual which can be given to each employee.

RESPONSIBILITY SCHEDULE

JOB TITLE: Workshop Foreman

IMMEDIATE SENIOR: Service Manager

IMMEDIATE SUBORDINATES: Workshop Supervisors

RESPONSIBLE FOR   (a)   Controlling the over-all standard of work.
                    (b)   Assisting with technical problems as necessary.
                    (c)   Controlling workshop discipline, and the detail of working conditions.
                    (d)   General cleanliness and tidiness of the workshop.
                    (e)   Allocation of special tools and equipment.
                    (f)   Direct control of training.
                    (g)   Ensuring harmonious relationships within the workshop and with other departments.
                    (h)   Taking steps to ensure that current legal requirements are met.

Fig. 2.6   Responsibility schedule

Span of Control (or 'Span of Management')

As the organization becomes divided up, a system of control must be devised and the basic management principle of 'span of control' must be borne in mind.

This span refers to the number of subordinates that a manager or supervisor can effectively control. In the past management writers have tended to stipulate a definite number of subordinates, usually five or six. In practice there are many variables which affect the effective span of control, the two main factors being the type of work involved and the personal abilities of both the superior and subordinates. Research shows that in practice the limits of span of control are elastic, and may vary from 2 to 15 people.

It is thus not practical to lay down general rules for determining the 'correct span of control' in all dealerships, or in different departments, but obviously the span must narrow at higher levels. For example, a dealership may have a large workshop which is handling one particular type of car, and where the Service Manager can effectively control a large group of workers. If the company is then appointed agent for a second make of car which is an expensive luxury model, it is quite possible that, although the total number of workers may not necessarily increase, the span of control may become too wide for one Service Manager. It may then be necessary to modify the organization structure, and to appoint, in addition to the existing Service Manager, a Service Manager for the repair of luxury cars. Such a step would allow mechanics to specialize, and would also give each Service Manager a realistic span of control. It should be stressed that the span only applies to management and supervisory levels. Too wide a span causes the superior to become overburdened and inefficient; too narrow a span creates more and more levels through which information must pass before a decision is taken, again causing inefficiency. Thus the ideal span will be a compromise between the two extremes.

CENTRALIZATION

In any business, large or small, control and decision-making can be limited to top management or can be delegated to the lower management levels. Absolute centralization is only possible in a one-man firm, since any sharing of work must involve at least a minimal amount of delegation. On the other hand complete decentralization would mean that everyone would be free to make his own decisions, and this would result in chaos. Therefore some degree of central control must exist.

Owing to various economic pressures such as the low rate of profit on capital invested and the need for increased capital expenditure, and because of changing patterns of service, recent years have seen the development of large motor trade groups, several of them now national companies. These groups have greater financial strength, and can thus operate more efficiently, and offer better services to the public. They have usually been formed by absorbing a number of garages into the parent group. This means that the basic structure consists of a head office, usually at a main dealership, and a group of satellite subsidiaries. An examination of the decision-making system in these groups will show either that top management decisions are made at head office and orders issued from the centre, or alternatively that each satellite operates as an autonomous unit responsible for its own profit or loss, with only limited guidance and control from head office.

The degree of centralization is a compromise, which depends on factors relating to the individual group, and in particular on the capabilities and attitudes of the Chief Executive. Over a period of many years most organizations oscillate between decentralization and centralization in response to the changing economic, financial, and technical pressures they encounter. The current general tendency is towards decentralization, with each unit operating under a General Manager and over-all control achieved by means of standard accounting and records methods and agreed budgets and objectives.

Advantages of Centralization

Standard control over the whole concern.
Economies in overheads and administration.
More efficient use of business machines and equipment.
More efficient use of specialists, e.g. in the fields of personnel, training, etc.

Disadvantages of Centralization

1. Strong central control can cause frustration at lower levels.
2. Lengthy lines of communication.
3. Increase in paperwork and reports.
4. Responsibilities and managerial experience at lower levels are reduced.
5. Decisions are taken at a distance from the place of application.

OBJECTIVES

These are goals or targets which an organization or sections within the organization try to achieve. Peter Drucker, the American management writer, has classified objectives as:

   (a) *General objectives* set by administration or higher management, which apply to the whole of the enterprise and tend to be long-term; and
   (b) *Specific objectives*, which are relatively less important, short-term, and usually apply to one department or section.

Although objectives may not be specified as such, they form part of the general policy of the company as formulated by the Board of Directors.

General objectives must be applicable to the particular organization. There are, however, three basic objectives which are taken as read and therefore not usually stated:

SURVIVAL. It is obvious that all dealerships intend to carry on trading in the future. This means that over a given period of time a 'break-even point' must be reached. This is the point at which the dealership has covered the cost of staying in business, revenues being equal to the sum total of rent, taxes, heating, lighting, wages, administrative expenses, and other overheads.

GROWTH. This does not necessarily mean actual increase in size, but rather that the dealership must move with the times and make full use of the latest operating, sales, marketing, and management techniques. This point is clearly illustrated if we compare the equipment necessary in a vehicle repair shop as recently as the late 1940s with the equipment necessary to offer an efficient service today.

PROFIT. Any firm must show a profit in order to remain in business. A Prices and Incomes Board report showed average profits in the motor trade to be 11 per cent, and even as low as 2 per cent in some service departments. These figures are clearly unacceptable, and can be placed in their proper perspective by looking at the profit figures for the large national motor groups. For example one group shows an annual profit of approximately £2·75 million, which is very healthy by any standard. The profit made must be large enough not merely to offset the effects of inflation but also either to provide future operating capital from retained earnings or to encourage further investment by share-holders. It is imperative that each department should show a profit. Some departments may run a section or offer a service which will not show a direct profit, e.g. free transport for customers leaving their cars; racing or sports cars sponsored by the garage; free service and check promotions. The cost of these activities must be included in the overheads of the departments concerned and recouped in this way. The earnings and costs of each department must be care-fully monitored; this is usually effected by means of budgetary control.

MANAGEMENT BY OBJECTIVES

This is a management technique developed in the U.S.A. Emphasis is placed on setting objectives for all parts of the organization, so that everyone is striving towards a target or targets for his particular job.

Basic Steps in Management by Objectives

1. Set general *targets for the dealership* as a whole. These can be based on past results; or in some cases are set in agreement with the manufacturer.
2. Set specific *targets for each department* which must be within, and in total make up, the dealership targets.
3. Set specific *targets for groups and individuals* within each department. At this stage, and at stage (2), workers, supervisors, and managers should be actively involved in setting targets. This will help to ensure that the targets are realistic, and that the targets which workpeople have to meet are their own targets, and therefore more acceptable than if they were imposed from above.
4. Design a *system of continuous checking* of actual results against the target set. This must show deviations quickly, but must not be so complex as to cause additional overheads in the form of clerical work. Wherever possible existing recording systems should be modified to incorporate targets. For example additional columns may be printed on the current job cards and time control sheets.
5. *Evaluate and modify targets* as necessary. It is important that targets present workers with a challenge, yet they must be realistic and possible to achieve. Modification will be necessary when targets are found to be unrealistic in practice, or when they become out of date for technical reasons. These five steps are shown in Fig. 2.7. Management by objectives is used in the following areas:

    vehicle sales   growth
    training   parts sales
    tyre, battery, accessory sales   service sales
    profit   employee productivity

Examples of objectives for four departments are shown in Fig. 2.8. Manu-

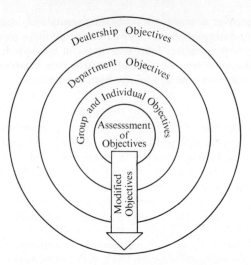

Fig. 2.7   Management by objectives

Department	Present Situation	Decision	Objective
SERVICE	10 technicians working a 40 hour week giving 40 × 10 = 400 hours labour available per week	To introduce a time-saving incentive scheme to increase sale of labour by 10 per cent	*To sell 400 + 10 per cent = 440 Labour Hours per week from June 1st 1980*
T.B.A.	Turnover £2000 per week	To increase turnover by 15 per cent over a specified period	*To increase turnover to £2000 + 15 per cent = £2300 per week by June 30th 1980*
PARTS	Stock classified as slow moving items valued at £15 000	To reduce the number of items classified as slow moving to 20 per cent less than current value	*To reduce the stock of parts classified as slow moving to £15000 − 20 per cent = £12 000 by 1980*
BODY REPAIR	Increasing volume of work. Work area inaccessible with very limited parking area	To relocate body-repair shop as a separate self-contained unit	*To open a large self-contained body-repair unit on the central industrial estate to cater for own and other trade customers by 1980*

N.B. The statements in column 3 are objective and easily measurable in that they state figures and dates. Objectives should not be written in general terms and phrases such as 'To ensure a satisfactory turnover' or 'To ensure that' must be avoided.

Fig. 2.8   Examples of objectives for four departments

facturers use objectives as a means of comparing agents' and dealers' performances on a national and regional basis. Put into operation, a practical system of Management by objectives will help a manager in his four basic functions of planning, co-ordinating, motivating and control (see Chapter 1) and help to obtain a higher return on both capital and human resources.

COMMITTEES

A committee has been described as 'a group of people sitting round a table discussing something', which probably is a good enough general definition to start with. The distinction between a committee and a meeting is that a committee is more formal, will have a prepared agenda, minutes of its discussions, and permanent or semi-permanent members, whereas a meeting is less formal and can be called at short notice, with informal discussion taking place as points of importance are raised. The use of committees and meetings in motor trade management is limited to the larger dealerships and groups for the simple reason that they are not needed where a small number of employees is involved. Since the tendency in recent years has been towards the formation of larger units, and this trend is likely to continue, committees and meetings are likely to be used more generally in future.

Types of Committee

Administrative. The Board of Directors is a committee representing the shareholders of a public company, and public service organizations are likewise directed by a Board. This type of committee is found in the larger motor trade groups where the Managing Director of each of the satellite dealerships holds a seat on the central Board of Directors. This central board deals with policy matters for the group as a whole and makes all major planning decisions.

Executive. This is usually made up of managers or head supervisors from different departments. Its basic function is to develop co-operation between the departments. A typical executive committee is made up of a Managing Director (chairman), General Manager, Company Secretary, Service Manager, Parts Department Manager, Vehicle Sales Manager, General Sales Manager, and Accountant.

Co-ordinating. This has a similar function to the executive committee but aims to achieve a higher degree of co-operation and harmony between departments by involving other interested parties than just the managers.

An *ad hoc* committee may be formed to deal with a particular topic and then disbanded when its work is complete. Decisions made by this type of committee do not carry the power of decisions made by the executive committee. An *ad hoc* committee is made up of persons representing all levels of the department concerned. One purpose served by this type of committee lies in the field of *communication*: a meeting can prove a useful method of passing information to a group, since it allows a two-way flow of information. An example is a meeting arranged at a time when a large garage has been appointed as an agent for a completely new car. The meeting allows a flow of information between representatives of the manufacturer and the agency. Persons attending this meeting could be: manufacturers' representatives (2); workshop foreman, workshop chargehand; technicians (2); mechanics (2); auto electrician, body repairer, paint sprayer, parts supervisors (2); partsmen (2); salesmen (2); accounts clerk.

Standing Committee. This is a permanent committee which is set up to supervise a specific function such as catering or the provision of welfare facilities. Members serving on these committees are often elected.

Consultative Committee. With this type of committee representatives of management and workers (unfortunate terms) are brought together. They usually deal with such matters as working conditions, wages and salaries, grievances, and current problems. This type of committee, properly organized and effectively operated, can create an atmosphere of co-operation and unity.

Joint Committee. This is a committee whose members represent the views and interests of two or more other committees. Again such committees can prove a great asset in developing co-operation.

Advantages of Committees

1. They are useful for co-ordinating the work of sections of departments.
2. Various ideas and views can be pooled for the benefit of all.
3. Committee members are forced to face up to problems.
4. Problems can be solved be discussion rather than by individuals tackling them alone.
5. Workers and supervisors can be involved in decisions affecting them.

Disadvantages of Committees

1. They can be time-wasting for the members.
2. They can be slow in reaching decisions.
3. The effectiveness of the committee depends very much on the chairman.
4. Responsibility for decisions rests with the committee and not with individuals. Members may vote for a decision that they would not have taken as individuals.
5. The effectiveness of a committee may be deliberately hindered by one or two members.

QUESTIONS

1. If you were to take over as a manager of an established family business with no formal management structure, how would you set about designing an organizational structure to ensure the smooth running of the business?
(I.M.I)
2. Explain the difference between managerial tasks and supervisory tasks in terms of the authority, responsibility, and accountability of each. (C. & G.)
3. Why is it important for companies to devise sound organization structures? If you were the managing director of a company, what circumstances would cause you to review critically the existing structure? (I.M.I.)
4. Distinguish between formal and informal organizations and explain why it is necessary to recognize both aspects of an organization. (I.M.I.)
5. 'The responsibilities of a Managing Director outside his company have increased, are increasing and should be increased still further.' Discuss.(I.M.I.)

6. Management by objectives has sometimes been criticised on the grounds that it creates more paperwork and form-filling, and so prevents a manager from 'getting on with the job'. How would you answer such a criticism? (I.M.I.)

7. 'Management by objectives demands that managers must state where the business stands now, where it wants to go, and how it is going to get there.' What are the main principles involved in operating a sound system of management by objectives? (M.A.A./I.M.I.)

8. Can a consultative committee ever be anything more than a complaints committee? (I.M.I.)

9. Draw up an organization chart for a service repair shop dealing with cars and commercial vehicles, and including body and paint repairs.
Use the chart to explain the difference between authority and responsibility. (C. & G.)

10. (a) What do you understand by the term 'organization structure'?
(b) If an organization is to work smoothly there must be adequate co-ordination. What are the main factors in co-ordination? (M.A.A./I.M.I.)

CHAPTER 3

PLANNING AND CONTROL

PLANNING

In Chapter one the general definition of the management function included planning, which was closely linked with control. These techniques, planning and control, are not confined to garage management but are a prerequisite of many activities in life. We could take annual holidays as an example; here many winter evenings may be spent studying brochures, arranging accommodation, or planning routes. This is the stage of collecting information and making plans. Once these plans have been made, certain financial objectives are set to cover the cost of the holiday; and so a control system, probably in the form of a bank account, is arranged to monitor progress towards those objectives over a limited period of time (before the holiday begins), and to ensure that those objectives are achieved in the time planned.

A few negatively-minded garage managers would claim, 'You cannot plan ahead in a business as fickle as ours'. This type of statement is evidence of a psychological rather than a practical barrier, since the very act of ordering itself constitutes a form of planning. Without planning, a dealership can only go from one immediate crisis to another.

Planning is a major part of the management process — one by which a manager looks for alternative courses of action and goals for the future. In explaining the basic need for planning, Fayol stated, 'Before taking any action it is *most* necessary to know what is possible and what is wanted' and 'Absence of a plan entails hesitations, false steps, and untimely changes of direction, which are causes of weakness if not disaster in business'.

Planning categories.

Planning categories used in the motor trade can be classified under three general headings. These are:

Corporate (long-term). This is the responsibility of top management, and involves the formulation of company policy and drawing up a master plan of what the dealership will achieve over a 5- to 10-year period. This type of planning is also referred to as 'strategic' planning, and deals with financial, economic, marketing, and growth aspects. It focuses attention on broad objectives, rather than defining precise goals.

Tactical (medium-term). This covers the systematic achievement of long-term plans, which must be translated from broad general objectives into detailed specific objectives. These specific objectives usually relate to the separate departments making up the dealership and in sum total form the long-term plans.

In both these types of planning the actual planning periods are not in isolated blocks of five years. Rather, at the end of each financial year the plan is projected forward a further year, thus maintaining a five-year onward-moving plan.

Operational (budget). This covers the week-by-week and month-by-month planning by both top management and departmental managers. Budgets are prepared by departmental managers well before the beginning of the financial year, and are then approved by the directors in accordance with the long-term plans. The agreed budget for the financial year can be divided to cover convenient periods of time or 'control periods' — often four-week periods or calender months. At the end of each control period a review of results is made, and corrective action taken where necessary. A budgetary system's basic aim is to control expenditure so that at all times income exceeds expenditure, but it also has indirect advantages, in that when managers are preparing their budget they are put in a position where they must plan realistically for the year ahead; and since the separate departmental budgets form the master budget, it initiates and encourages co-operation between sections and departments. Planning takes on increasing importance as the size of the dealership increases. While the manager of a small garage may devote little time to planning, a large motor-trade group will make use of specialist planners. Whatever the size of the organization the basic planning requirements are nevertheless present.

FORECASTING

This is an integral part of planning, and covers various methods of assessing probable future events. Forecasting is usually applied to such factors as:

development of premises;
sales targets;
special promotions;
charge-out rates.

Managers at all levels are required as part of their duty to appraise possibilities. This may be an informal appraisal; or it may involve the formal collection of information and the use of statistical analysis, however basic and unsophisticated. Since any motor-trade organization exists to meet the requirements of its customers, any forecasting is basically answering the question, 'Who will our customers be, and what services will they require?' Customer demand for service, and more particularly sales, shows movements or variations over a period of time — movements which are usually linked with the national economy. These trends can be found by analysing past figures. A simple analysis can be done by averaging figures for a past period of time; or alternatively the figures can be plotted on a graph, giving a pictorial representation. The curve of the graph can then be extended or projected to show probable future figures. These figures represent probabilities if conditions remain the same, and can be modified to take into account future national and regional demands. Information to assist in forecasting can be obtained at a national level from the publications of the major motor-trade organizations (see Chapter 6); from the National Economic

Development Council; or from vehicle manufacturers. At a regional or local level information can be gleaned by contacts with the M.A.A., or by operating an intelligence service on major competitors or specialist repairers and suppliers, and on their advertising techniques. Much general information is also available from local authorities and libraries.

Types of planning

Financial. Because of the complex nature of financial operations effective planning is all-important. Basic needs for any type of motor retail business are a continuing sound financial structure; the provision of realistic working capital; increasing capital earnings to provide for expansion; and the improvement of services offered. These are the major responsibilities of the Board of Directors or Proprietors, together with their specialist financial advisors. Short-term financial planning involves all personnel from supervisory level upwards. The usual form of planning is through the process of budgeting. The basic system for the preparation of budgets is shown in Fig. 3.1. The type of budgeting system employed will reflect the organizational structure. Some dealerships limit the use of budgets to cost control only, in which case expenses for each department are considered. Others employ 'budgetary control' as a true management tool, to plan the level of activity in each department as well as to control income *and* expenses. Any form of budgeting, as well as ensuring financial control, provides a secondary benefit in that the process of constructing the budget tends to bring an understanding between departments, and helps to generate a sense of unity in the dealership.

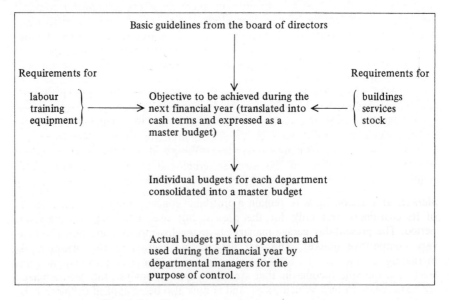

Fig. 3.1   Basic stages in budget preparation

Profit. The prime objective of a motor-trade business is to find new clients and to keep the regular customers. This ensures the prosperity of the business and a profit for the owners or shareholders. Planning and control of profit is a major aspect of effective management, since net profit is a measure of the over-all effectiveness of the enterprise. As with other types of planning, arriving at a profit target involves the predetermination of future customer demand, services offered, and the cost of operations. Because targets are based on variables, it is unrealistic to express profit as a definite figure unless a variance is allowed. Therefore a target is usually expressed as £10 000 gross plus or minus 15 per cent. Better still, the target should be related to the funds employed: e.g. 'by 1980 gross profit will show a return on funds of 20 per cent over-all'. The profit objective should be seen as a way of life rather than an actual sum of money.

Manpower. In the early development of a motor trade establishment, manpower planning is limited to ensuring that the expertise and skills necessary to cover all aspects of the business are available. In many instances several areas of responsibility can be covered by one person. As the business expands the jobs involved become more varied and specialized. This increase in the number of separate activities will require more complex systems of organization and control, and the staff involved will need more specialized skills. The purpose of manpower planning is to foresee the future staff requirements. If the manpower plan is to be reasonably accurate it must be based on an accurate forecast of the development of the dealership as a whole. For this reason the corporate long-term plans must be expressed in terms of personnel at all levels, as well as in terms of capital, sales, and physical expansion.

There are several forms of manpower planning, including complex mathematical models, but these are usually only practical where personnel specialists are dealing with large numbers of employees. Motor-trade practice is to base manpower requirements directly on the forecast level of sales and service, taking into account expected changes in marketing and service methods and expansion or development plans. For example when a 5-year plan is drawn up for the service department it may include an extension of the workshop area based on an expected increase of 15 per cent in service requirements. When the layout of the extended workshop has been finalized, the required number of technicians, semi-skilled operators, and ancillary workers can readily be calculated. The result of this calculation must then be developed in terms of staff development, recruiting, and training. Changes in services offered and in methods of marketing inevitably mean changes in the numbers employed and in the ratios of the required skills, which must reflect the changing face of the retail motor trade.

Market. If a dealership is to remain a profitable concern it must serve the needs of its customers, not only for the present but over the long-term planning period. The present-day garage manager is 'managing money', and doing so in a very competitive market. The real determining factors in the planning of marketing schemes are the total vehicle population in a given area and the true level of disposable income in that area. This type of analysis has been applied for some years to new vehicle sales, and is now also being applied to the service department; the term 'service marketing' has been added to the motor-trade vocabulary.

Development. A dealership must move with the times: it cannot afford to stand still. This type of planning is referred to by some manufacturers as 'dealer development'. It is obviously closely allied to market and financial planning. Development looks to the future, and to future demands. The increasing vehicle population, increasing service intervals, and legislation relating to vehicle safety are demanding a different pattern of service. Most dealerships face ever-increasing overheads and labour costs, and some have moved out of city centres to low-rated areas. Many are operating or are planning specialist repair sections; diagnostic bays; 'while you wait' and 'predetermined time' services; improved reception and waiting facilities; and merchandizing areas. These factors demand investment in new or modified buildings and in sophisticated and expensive equipment, both of which will reduce the labour content in costs and improve quality. And all of this demands long-term financial and practical planning based on market research.

CONTROL

This is a term often viewed with suspicion by new management students and by organized labour. In its true context it is the second logical step in the planning process. At the planning stage policies, aims, or objectives are set; control is the process that gauges present performance against what was planned. Both processes are therefore inter-linked and make a vital contribution to the efficiency of any dealership or group – and indeed are necessary to ensure survival. Control can be classified as external, that is, control exercised by government legislation, vehicle manufacturers, or trade organizations; and internal, that is control exercised by using budgets, standard costs, time records, balance sheets and accounts relating to the dealership itself.

Principles of Control

1. The system of controls used must be tailored to suit the particular organization's structure. In a small garage a relatively simple system will be adequate, whereas a large dealership will of necessity require a comprehensive system.
2. The end-product of the control system used in each department should integrate easily with those of other departments to form an over-all control system.
3. Each section should be organized by arranging practical objectives in such a way as to be, as far as is practical, 'self-controlling'.
4. The actual system should be as simple and straightforward as possible, with a direct link between the controller and controlled. This ensures that the system is understood by the people concerned and is effective.
5. The system should be based on a series of 'key points' rather than being applied to each detailed operation. This is a practical application of F.W. Taylor's 'principle of exception'. The 'key points' are usually based on the major operations carried out in a department. Identification of these 'key points' produces a system that is simple, cost-effective, and flexible.
6. When results vary from what is planned the system should automatically trigger off some form of corrective action.

7. Most control systems involve people, and the human factor must be taken into account in devising the system. A system may be technically good, but mày not be acceptable to the workers involved. To a large extent psychological barriers can be avoided by involving personnel themselves in the design or selection of the system. There are several proprietary control systems available which can be tailored to the requirements of a particular dealership or department. An example of standardized control documentaiton is shown in Fig. 3.2(a) and 3.2(b).

As stated earlier, the basic objective of an enterprise is survival. This means that in real terms it must cover the cost of being in business; which means that revenue from all activities must, at a very minimum, cover the total operating cost of the business, the difference between total costs and revenue being net profit. This net profit must be apportioned between taxation, retention for use in the dealership to provide for growth, and return on the capital invested by proprietors or shareholders. An important aspect of profitability is the accurate control and classification of costs. The usual general classifications used are:

Fixed costs. Fixed costs are those which are automatically incurred without relation to the level of activity in the dealership.

Variable costs; These are related directly to the volume of work and will normally rise with an increase in activity.
These are further sub-divided into:

Direct Costs. These can be directly related to an activity or operation; the major direct cost is wages.

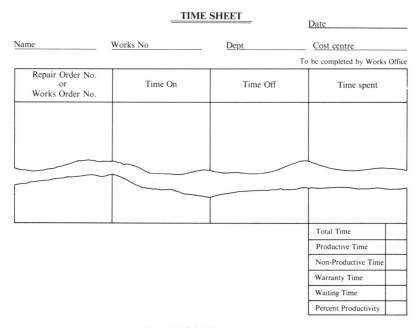

Fig. 3.2(a) Time sheet

CHURCH ROAD MOTORS

CAPITAL EXPENDITURE BUDGET PROPOSAL

Department____Service____   Financial Year/Period____198X__

Item or Project	Reasons	Prio-rity	Cash Price (£)	Annual Savings (£)	Service Life (years)	Annual Depreciation (£)
Electronic engine analyser	Old unit defective and obsolete – new unit to form centre-piece of two-bay diagnostic centre.	A	2500	900	5–7	300
Argon arc welding unit	To reduce welding and stripping time on body repairs; and to improve quality of work. Possible 15–20 per cent increase in profit.	B	700	350–400	10	50
Pneumatic brake bleeding unit	Problems encountered when bleeding brakes on 1300 and 1500 models.	A	150	80	7	20
On-car wheel balancer	Present unit only capable of static balancing. Dynamic balancing necessary.	C	800	200	5	100

Fig. 3.2(b) Capital budget proposal

Indirect Costs. These are costs which are not incurred by any particular operation, but by the dealership as a whole, e.g. administration costs.

	DIRECT COSTS	INDIRECT COSTS
FIXED	Rent and rates Wages of non-productive staff Costs of basic services e.g. lighting Service contracts for equipment	Depreciation of buildings Administration and B.O.D. expenses Insurance
VARIABLE	Operators' wages Department expenses Parts handling	Advertising

This gives a system of classifying costs in general terms. In practice the process of classification is complicated by costs which fall under two classifications. For example the costs of electrical power has to be divided between general lighting for workshop and forecourt, which is fixed, and power used to operate equipment, which increases with the volume of work and is variable. Under these conditons a manager must identify a basis for additional classifications, or decide on the percentage of fixed and variable cost from past experience. Whichever method is used, a clear distinction must be made between the total of fixed and the total of variable costs.

Larger dealerships break down total costs by using cost centres, so that expenditure can be identified with its source. Cost centres are usually based on departments and sections within the departments.

Break-even charts. The relationship between revenue and costs can be represented in a visual form by a break-even chart. In its simplest form it consists of a straight line representing total revenue and a second straight line representing total costs, the point of intersection being the break-even point. Such a chart is valuable because it shows the relationship between the level of activity and the costs and profit related to it. It can be seen from Fig. 3.3 that because of fixed costs no profit can be made until a certain volume of work is reached. Once the break-even point is reached profits increase more rapidly than total costs. The practical value is that the effect of any change in costs or revenue on profit can be clearly illustrated by modifying the chart. The manager can then see the effect of any decision he makes, before he implements it.

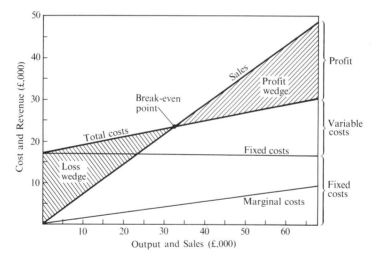

Fig. 3.3   Break-even chart

To refer again to Fig. 3.3, if fixed costs were increased the fixed cost line would be lifted, which would in turn lift the variable cost line, giving a higher break-even point. Marginal costs are the variable costs attributed directly to a product or service, the marginal costs added to the fixed costs giving the total costs. The difference between the marginal cost and selling price of a product is termed the contribution, since it contributes to the total profit.

One particular type of graph used for purposes of comparison is the Z chart, which shows figures or values on a time base. As the name implies, the three curves of the graph approximately form a letter Z. The curves are monthly totals shown as a single black line; cumulative monthly totals shown as a double black line; and a moving annual total shown as a single black line. The Z chart shown in Fig. 3.4(a) is based on the figures shown in the table, Fig. 3.4(b). When a number of charts for consecutive periods are placed 'end on' (Fig. 3.5) the trend is shown by the continuous moving annual total.

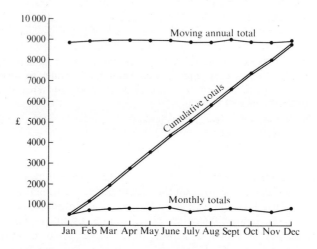

Fig. 3.4(a) Z Chart

	£ 1976	£ 1977	Cumulative total	Moving annual total
January	450	500	500	8750
February	650	700	1200	8800
March	700	750	1950	8850
April	800	800	2750	8850
May	800	800	3550	8850
June	850	820	4370	8820
July	700	650	5020	8770
August	750	750	5770	8770
September	700	800	6570	8870
October	850	750	7320	8770
November	700	650	7970	8720
December	750	800	8770	8770

Fig. 3.4(b)

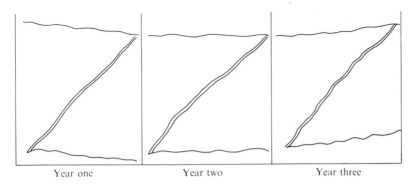

Year one   Year two   Year three

Fig. 3.5   When charts for consecutive years are placed together the general
            trend is shown by the moving annual total line. In year one the
            figures are falling; in year two they are at a constant level; and year
            three shows a steady rise.

BUDGETARY CONTROL

Under the heading 'financial planning', budgets were drawn up for each
department which combined to form the master budget. During the year departmental managers use these budgets in order to run a continuous comparison of
actual and budgeted figures. Budgetary control can be usefully applied to all but
the smallest garage; and here the proprietor has direct personal control and in
fact practises budgetary control mentally. The person preparing the budget must

CHURCH ROAD MOTORS

BUDGET REPORT

BUDGET CENTRE   Service Dept B2   BUDGET PERIOD   8

Section	Current Period			Year to date		
	Allowed Cost £	Actual Cost £	Variance	Allowed Cost £	Actual Cost £	Variance
Repair	100	110	+ 10	800	750	− 50
Body Repair	80	75	− 5	640	600	− 40
Electrical						
Servicing						
Diagnostic						
I.C.E.						
TOTALS						

Fig. 3.6   Budget report form. Shows an allowed budget for the mechanical
            repair department of £1300 per 13-period financial year. Figures for
            each department would be entered for each control period, giving
            continuous control.

ensure that it reflects expected targets for the coming year and does not become 'a repetition of last year's figures plus 15 per cent'. It is usual practice for the manager who prepares the budget to be responsible for actual performance. Each department or budget centre will keep a detailed record of all probable costs by means of, initially, a cost ledger book and, later, a budget report form, Fig. 3.6 shows a typical example. The reports from each department are combined and presented to the Managing Director as a summary of the master budget, as shown in Fig. 3.7. The variance column is the most crucial section. Any large variations must be carefully investigated.

CHURCH ROAD MOTORS

MASTER BUDGET SUMMARY

Budget Period _____

Month to Date				Year to Date		
Allowed Cost	Actual Cost	Variance	Budget Centre	Allowed Cost	Actual Cost	Variance
			B1 Vehicle Sales			
			B2 Service			
			B3 Parts			
			B4 Forecourt			
			B5 T.B.A.			
			B6 Office			
			TOTAL COSTS			

Fig. 3.7   Budget summary

Since some costs are outside the direct control of the manager because of inflationary trends and the volume of work, some flexibility can be built into the figures, with the actual variance controlled by the Managing Director or Financial Executive.

Control is necessary at all levels in a dealership. The system must be adequate for the purpose, without being too costly to operate or over-complicated.

DATA PROCESSING

The effective operation of both planning and control systems depends to a large extent on processing some form of data. Simple examples are individual customer accounts, service records, employees' wages, stock levels, and ordering. More complex examples are company accounts, balance sheets, profit records, and the preparation of figures for decision-making using statistical methods.

There are several methods used for processing these figures. A person handling data makes use of his brain, which is a form of complex computer. In order to increase the speed of operation some assistance is usually provided. This can take the form of simple tables, such as percentage-discount or compound-interest tables, but more often takes the form of some of the following equipment.

ADDING/LISTING MACHINES. These consist of mechanical keys which print on to a paper roll so that, as additions and subtractions are made from the keyboard, all figures, totals, and subtotals are recorded. Such machines may function either by lever operation or electrically. For forecourt work this type of machine can be incorporated in a cash register. It is extremely useful for providing a permanent record of figures automatically.

ELECTRONIC CALCULATORS. These have been in use since the early sixties and are completely electronic. Figures are 'keyed in' by simple touch keys, the four basic arithmetic functions are performed instantaneously, and results are displayed by electronic display digits. Calculators for business use can also be equipped with a percentage key, one or more memories, and a print-out roll.

ACCOUNTING MACHINES. These are, in effect, a combined typewriter and adding machine, and are used for repetitive jobs such as updating stock records, sales ledgers, and payrolls, or for any other jobs which involve taking up a previous balance, recording a debit or credit, and recording a new balance. Most machines print the account sheet and also a summary or proof sheet. More sophisticated machines of this type have facilities for more complex calculations, information storage, and simple programming.

CARD SYSTEMS. Card systems of many different types are used to store information. They can be divided into two groups, the first being a system in which the details are written or typed on a standard form and placed in an index which allows rapid retrieval of the information required, usually by means of a special cabinet. The second and more complex type is a punch card system, where the card is divided into columns and figures or letters are represented by holes punched in the card by either a hand punch or a key punch machine similar to a typewriter. The information is then verified or checked for accuracy and the cards sorted or filed. The information can be read by a tabulator, which in its more complex forms can be programmed to carry out mathematical functions, calculate totals and sub-totals, and give a print-out. This type of system was the most effective method of handling data before the advent of electronic computers.

COMPUTERS. The earliest computers were used primarily for processing complicated scientific calculations. The possibility of adapting them for business use was at first overlooked. In the main the impact of the computer on the retail motor-trade has been through the manufacturers, which means that a normal retail outlet is only indirectly involved, in that it supplies information to 'feed' the computer and has processed information returned to it. It must be remembered that a computer is a tool of management and not 'the manager'. It is an electronic device that will operate as instructed by its program. The main advantages of computers are:

Speed. A computer can perform any mathematical function, store information, and produce results in a fraction of a second.

Storage. A computer has the capacity to store large quantities of data in a small space and, equally important, the capacity to gain access very rapidly. It can also update data very quickly.

Accuracy. All data will be processed with total accuracy, provided that the input data are accurate and the computer is programmed correctly.

Planning. A computer can be invaluable in planning and forecasting, since it can show the effects of making changes.

Control. A computer makes the use of more control areas practical, since greater volumes of data can be processed than would be possible using normal clerical methods.

A computer cannot think for itself. It will carry out the operations for which it has been programmed. It cannot therefore handle unexpected events outside its program, and is not the mystical 'black box' often portrayed in fiction. A computer consists of five basic units, as shown in Fig. 3.8.

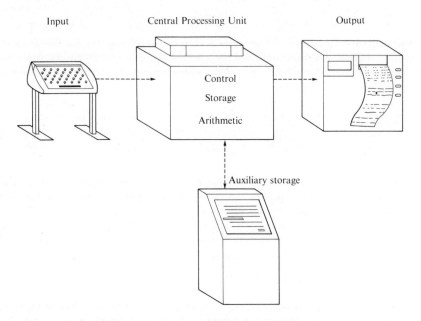

Fig. 3.8   The basic units of a computer

Input. This is the device by which instructions and data are transferred to the computer. The information must be in a computer language. The input unit converts this language into electrical impulses.

Storage. The instructions and data are passed from the input to the storage or memory unit, where electrical impulses activate magnetic or semiconductor memory units, and are held in this form until required. The instructions are thus held in readiness and can trigger off a sequence of operations, so that the computer can operate automatically through a program of complex or repetitive calculations without a human operator. Since this part of the computer is expensive, alternative forms of storage can be used. These are usually termed auxiliary or backing stores, and take the form of punched cards, magnetic tape similar to that used on tape recorders, or discs similar to long-playing records.

Arithmetic. The computer can carry out basic arithmetic functions and compare the results on a go/no-go basis. Since the operations are carried out electronically, thousands of calculations can be carried out in a fraction of a second.

Control. This unit interprets the instructions in the program in a strict sequence, and controls the circuitry so as to route the data to the various units to give the required results. The storage, arithmetic, and control units form the Central Processing Unit or the computer proper.

Output. This performs the reverse process to the input unit in translating from the machine language into a language which can be understood by humans. The output can take the form of printed sheets, punched tape, or a visual display similar to a television screen.

CRITERIA FOR USING COMPUTERS. The use of a computer can be extremely costly. This is due not only to the cost of the computer and its associated equipment, but also to the cost of the necessary planning and modification of the organizational, communication, and decision-making systems. Some form of feasibility study is imperative before a computer system is considered. In the majority of dealerships some of the systems described above, such as accounting machines and card systems, will be quite competent and cost-effective in coping with routine work. The use of a computer would generally be considered when there are:

(a) a large volume of data as input or output, particularly data of a repetitive nature such as accounts, wages, or stock-control and ordering data;

(b) work which employs a large non-productive clerical staff, such as inventory-control, cash-flow, market research;

(c) areas of work where planning or control have proved very difficult.

ACQUIRING COMPUTER SERVICES. It is doubtful if any single dealership could fully utilize even a modest computer installation. In a large group a central computer which can be connected with several terminals at different locations can be used. If a computer is found to be justified it must be used to the maximum if it is to be cost-effective. The ideal arrangement would be to reorganize the flow of information in the group and to use the computer to cover as many areas of work as possible, so as to give a fully integrated system. A computer installation can be purchased outright or can be rented or leased. It is cheaper in the long term to buy outright, but after 10 − 15 years the installation is obsolete. Renting or leasing ensures up-to-date equipment and spreads the cost over a period of time. The factors involved, including finance, tax considerations, operational costs, staffing, the future expansion of the group, etc., are so numerous and complex it would be an advantage to use a computer to assist in decision-making!

An alternative is to use a computer bureau. This is an external organization which offers computer services for hire. Two alternative methods of processing data are generally available. In the first, data are prepared and posted to the bureau, which processes them on its computer and returns them to the dealership. The alternative, which gives greater flexibility but is more costly, is to hire a terminal installation which is connected by a telephone line to the bureau's computer. A bureau can provide the answer to data processing where there is insufficient work to warrant owning a computer or where peaks in the work, such as accounts and stock orders, occur. It avoids the high capital investment and the less obvious running costs of owning a computer, and offers immediate expertise at a predictable cost. An example of part of a bureau service is shown in Fig. 3.9(a) and (b). This system is currently being used very effectively by many major franchises for Parts Department stock control. In outline the system relies on the use of a simple translucent record card, Fig. 3.9(a), which is retained on the premises. Input data is sent to the bureau in the form of either a magnetic tape cassette or dyeline copies of the cards. This information is forwarded by Data post, a service operated by the Post Office. The bureau processes the data and returns the following:

Weekly   Movement reports
                              Recommended order list
                              Management report

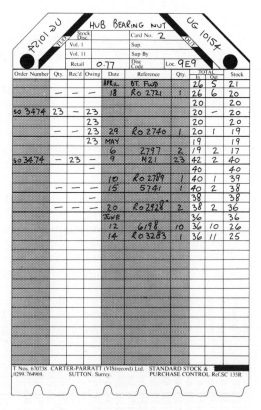

Fig. 3.9(a) Parts record card

Part Number	Description	Qty	Rec	Owed	In	Out	Stk	Ave Wk Sale	6 Mnth	Lost No	Sale Qty	C	R	UOI	Rec Ord	Remarks
13H 6380	Clip											N	0	Ten		New part number
13H 6384	Sidelamp			5	7	4	3	1.36	26			B	0			New bin location
13H 6385	Sidelamp			18	3	2	1	1.63	31			B	0		6	
13H 6394	Lamp assy			2	2	1	1	.36	7			D	0			
13H 6395	Lamp assy				3	1	2	.42	8			D	0		2	
13H 6396	Lamp assy		9		12		12	1.73	33			A	0		7	Auto Cat Change
13H 6404	Lamp assy				8	1	7	.15	3			t	0			
13H 6436	Lamp assy				2		1	.10	2			t	0	Ten		
13H 6461	Fastener		3		82	20	62	4.78	91			J	0			
13H 6467	Switch				6		6	.47	9			D	0	Ten		
13H 6473	Foot valve				12		12	.10	2			J	0			Check Stock Card
13H 6475	Pump			5	15	5	10	1.68	32			B	0			
13H 6480	Lamp assy				4	1	3	.36	7			D	0			Check Stock Card
13H 6692	Jack handle	1	2	1	2		2	.31	6			D	0			
13H 6744	Brake hose											H	1			S/S by 83H DNR Check Stock Card Not for Reorder
13H 6823	Clutch cyl				4	1	3	.36	7			D	0			Auto Cat Change
13H 6862	Seal				168	6	162	9.31	177			J	0	Ten		
13H 6956	Wrning swtch				18	1	17	1.10	21			B	0			
13H 7083	Pop out unit				7	4	3	.73	14			C	0		5	New Bin location
13H 7109	Lighter		5		9	1	8	.78	15			C	0			Auto Cat change
13H 7352	Speedo mph				4	3	1	.57	11			D	0			
13H 7370	Choke cable				12	4	8	1.21	23			B	0		5	
13H 7618	Therm switch		6		7		7	.68	13			C	0		5	
13H 7759	Light switch				27	1	26	2.78	53			A	0	Fve		

DATE 05 09 75 — DISTRIBUTOR 00 — MOVEMENT REPORT — SHEET 38

Fig. 3.9(b) Parts movement report

Monthly	Bin price list
Half-yearly	Stock valuation and summary
On request	Selective printouts

Fig. 3.9(b) shows a movement report, one of the printouts returned to the dealership. This gives a complete picture of the parts movements enjoyed by the Parts Department in the preceding weeks, and includes the following types of information:

Quantity	–	ordered, received, owed
Quantity	–	stocked, sold, balance remaining
Average weekly sale	–	per part
Sales 6 months to date	–	per part
Lost Sale Data (As occurring and cumulative)	–	per stocked part
Category or part	–	per non-stocked part
Redundancy code or part	–	related to sales history.

Remarks column including:

Check stock card	Deleted from stock file, superseded by:
No master record	
New part number	Not for re-order
New bin location	Now for re-order
Lost sale data	Category change
New price	Auto category change
Sales amendment	Redundancy code change
Master delete	Now nil stock

This service is backed up by regular visits to the dealership by experienced systems consultants with motor-trade experience, who can offer general assistance and record each visit on a standard report form.

GLOSSARY OF COMPUTER TERMS

Because a whole new series of terms have developed with computers and associated equipment, some are listed below for reference.

Ancillary equipment. This is any data-processing equipment which is not directly controlled or connected to the main computer, such as key punch equipment.

Batch processing. This is where all the data of a particular type are accumulated and processed as a 'batch' at a particular time of the week or month.

Bureau. A Bureau is an organization which hires out the facilities of a comprehensive computer service to outside companies.

Central processing unit (c.p.u.) This is the heart of the computer system. It is the equipment which carries out arithmetic and immediate storage.

Cobol. This is a computer language used in particular for programming business data. It makes use of letters, numbers, and symbols. Cobol is a word formed from the initial letters of COmmon Business-Oriented Language.

Electronic data processing (e.d.p.). This is the use of any electronic machine which processes data.

Fortran. This is a language used mainly for scientific work.

Hardware. This refers to any of the mechanical/electronic devices which form part of a computer installation, including such items as the central processing unit, card reader, and printer.

Integrated data processing. This is a system of storing data in a common bank or pool which can be used for different but related purposes, e.g. car sales, servicing, and customer records.

In-house. This refers to a computer installation which is located in the dealership or group. The installation can be owned, rented, or leased.

Market Research. This is an analysis of marketing figures in order to determine future potential.

Peripheral equipment. This is equipment which is controlled by and connected to the central processing unit.

Package. This is a set of pre-prepared programmes which can be purchased to carry out specific tasks.

Program. A program is a series of instructions issued in a correct sequence to the computer, to give a particular result.

Random access. This is a method of storing information so that it can be retrieved in any required sequence.

Real Time Processing. This makes possible an immediate two-way communication between the terminal and the c.p.u. and storage system.

Sequential access. This is where information can only be retrieved in a given sequence.

Software. These are the smaller items such as tapes, punched cards, etc., which form part of the control system. They are the consumable items.

Stand-by facility. This is an arrangement made with an external organization to use their computer in the event of a breakdown.

Storage. This forms the memory of the computer. Immediate storage is achieved electronically in the c.p.u. but is limited by costs. Backing storage can be achieved in a separate machine using punched tape, magnetic tape, or magnetic discs.

Systems analyst. A specialist who determines the most effective procedures for problem-solving (usually including data-processing) is known as a systems analyst.

Time sharing. This is a system which involves using a central unit which processes a number of terminals at random times.

Validation. The process of checking the instructions in a computer program is known as validation.

QUESTIONS

1. Clearly define what you understand by the term 'Control'. Discuss the different forms and methods of control you would implement as the manager of a medium-sized garage. (I.M.I.)

2. Why is forecasting important to a company? How could the management of a firm in the motor industry attempt to forecast future business? (I.M.I.)

3. Given the estimated monthly trading profit of a service repair department, what Daily Control System could be introduced to show day-by-day progress towards monthly break-even point? (C. & G.)

4. (a) What is meant by a 'departmental budget' and how is it prepared? (b) What is 'budgetary control' and how is it used to control workshop costs and profitability? (I.M.I.)

5. State the factors which would influence your choice in using EITHER a computer bureau service OR a card system for the control of parts stock. (C. & G.)

CHAPTER 4

COMMUNICATIONS

In a management context the term 'communication' refers to the flow of information necessary to enable an organization to function. The communications system can be likened to the flow of blood in the human body. This is a good analogy since the flow of information in an organization is as important to its well-being as the flow of blood is to the well-being of the body. It is vital that known and effective communications links should exist among all departments making up the dealership, the various sections within the departments, and each individual working in those sections. Information of many different types must pass continually up, down, and across the dealership structure, as well as to outside bodies such as suppliers, manufacturers, and customers.

Poor communications can be a real problem as a dealership expands. A small garage with a proprietor and two or three employees can have an effective system of communications functioning through nothing more than a note-pad and a desk diary. As the business expands and becomes more diversified personal contact becomes impracticable, more people are involved in transmitting information, and a definite system must be devised to match the organizational structure. The importance of communications cannot be over-emphasized. Poor communications lead to poor co-operation between departments, resulting in poor over-all dealership performance and profitability and increased customer and employee dissatisfaction.

CHANNELS OF COMMUNICATION

These are the routes along which information passes. The 'chain of command' as shown on the organization chart indicates the official channels of communication which, as a general rule, run in vertical lines up and down the organization, usually from the Managing Director or General Manager to the Service Manager, Parts Manager, Sales Manager, and Office Manager, and then downwards through the supervisors in each department. In addition there must be lines of communication running across the organization between different departments or sections. These are termed lateral communications. An example of this would be a memo from the Sales Manager to the Parts Manager.

UNOFFICIAL CHANNELS OF COMMUNICATION

In practice some pieces of information do not flow through the official channels described above but are passed by word of mouth from friend to friend, often between different levels and between different departments, so that the official channels are 'short-circuited'. The unofficial channels are commonly known as 'the grapevine' and, if it were possible to show them in the form of a chart, they could be superimposed on the official channels shown on the organization chart. A manager must accept the grapevine as a natural result of contact between individuals and groups who work together. It is found in organizations such as clubs and associations, as well as in the working environment. An enlightened manager will make effective use of both the official and unofficial channels of communication. The grapevine can be used when it is necessary to pass information quickly, for example in order to dispel unfounded rumours.

Some managers see the grapevine as a challenge; but it need only be viewed in this light if information does not pass freely in all directions and at all levels. The grapevine then becomes more active, but the information it passes may well be based on odd bits of information read from confidential memos, or overheard on the telephone, and these snippets of information form the basis for conjecture and rumours which in the long run cause unrest and uncertainty among the employees. If this type of situation is to be avoided then clearly all managers have a responsibility to ensure that *all* employees are supplied with accurate and up-to-date information, particularly in relation to matters affecting jobs, working conditions, working procedures, and company policy. Depending on the size of the dealership this may be done by word of mouth, notices posted on notice-boards, letters, or a regular newsheet. These procedures will ensure that the grapevine will not compete with the official system of communication, but will rather help in maintaining a stable and highly motivated work-force who feel that they 'belong'.

BASIC ELEMENTS OF COMMUNICATION

Communication occurs in five stages, as shown in Fig. 4.1. Most types of communication make use of *words*, either written or spoken. Words are symbols which may represent an object, or an action, or a person's feelings. The interpretation of words may vary from one person to another, depending on their educational and social backgrounds, as well as the locality in which each was brought up. In attempting to communicate a manager or supervisor will often find that the person receiving the message takes the words in a different sense from that which was intended. The extent of this problem can be illustrated by glancing at random at a good dictionary and noting the number of meanings that a single word can have in common usage. To overcome this problem the originator of the message must take care in the wording to ensure that this meaning is clear, precise, and unambiguous. The recipient must read or listen carefully and try to understand the meanings of individual words in the context of the message as a whole. If the contents of a communication are vitally important the sender can double-check by asking for feedback from the recipient.

TYPES OF COMMUNICATION

SPOKEN WORD. This is a major form of communication for both managers and supervisors, and is used in discussions, at meetings, and to issue instructions. The advantages of the spoken word are that a relationship is developed between

STAGE 1	INFORMATION SOURCE	Sender desires to impart information to another person or group of people
STAGE 2	ENCODING	Sender decides on some form of message: speech, writing, gesture, sketch, etc.
STAGE 3	TRANSMISSION	Message is transmitted by voice, handwriting, typing, physical gesture, etc.
STAGE 4	RECEPTION	Person or group receives message, i.e. hears, reads, sees message.
STAGE 5	DECODING	Recipient tries to grasp the meaning of the message and places his own interpretation on it.

Fig. 4.1   The basic communication process

the people involved; emphasis can be placed on certain phrases by use of voice and facial expressions; the speaker has an immediate indication of the recipient's response; mistakes can be rectified immediately; and decisions can be reached quickly and effectively.

Its main disadvantage lies in the fact that there is no permanent record of what was said; it can also be time-consuming if large numbers of people are involved or if the speaker is side-tracked into irrelevant conversation, and mistakes can be made because normally less care and forethought is used than would be the case in a written communication. A subtle form of communication which can be classified under this heading is 'silence', which can show displeasure if used during conversation. It is important that the recipient is aware of the reason for the silence, and is not left in 'silent doubt'. As well as the actual words used in oral communications the speaker's general appearance, tone of voice, facial expression, and gestures play a vital part in 'getting the message over'.

TELEPHONE. The telephone is used in a dealership for both internal and external communications. It provides an immediate form of communication without the need for a personal meeting. It is often cheaper to make a telephone call than to prepare and post a letter; but nevertheless it must be borne in mind that each individual call increases the telephone bill. In order to make efficient use of the telephone care must be exercised in dialling or recording numbers. Documents or notes required to make the call should be to hand, and the message should be brief, clear, and courteous. The person making calls or answering the telephone represents the dealership to the outside world, and the switchboard operator plays a very important part in the public and customer relations of any motor-trade establishment. An efficient switchboard operator with a pleasing personality and a sound knowledge of the dealership organization can do much to enhance its image. Training of operators is undertaken by the Post Office.

MEMORANDA. These are used as a major form of internal communication in a dealership. A memorandum has the advantage over the spoken word that it can be filed and can act as a permanent record (the message is usually typed). It is passed from one individual or department to another. The effectiveness of memos depends on the system used within the dealership or group for handling them, and most trade organizations use their own standard memo form. The features of a good memo are:

BELVEDERE GARAGES GROUP

REF. NO. 30/JR/LK   *DATE   5th SEPT. 1976*

Technical College Attendance

FROM   Training Officer   *TO   All Managers*

Copies To.
General Manager
Service Manager
Parts Manager
Office Manager

Arrangements have been made with the Heads of Department concerned for the following apprentices and trainees to attend Westbridge College of Technology on the days shown. This is in addition to the attendance at Westbridge Automotive Training Centre noted on memo 26/AS/LK for service and parts personnel.

Monday	J. Baldwin
	S. Brown
	L. Shepherd
	R. Allison
Tuesday	R. March
Wednesday	S. Norman
	D.G. Bates
Thursday	T. Cummins
Friday	L. Bakewell
	R. Turpin
	J.G. Walker
	B. Gibson

J. Raper

J. Raper   Group Training Officer.

Fig. 4.2   Format of a memorandum

(a)   title of sender and recipients
(b)   clear indication of subject matter (title)
(c)   a reference number
(d)   date
(e)   brief but comprehensive and courteous wording
(f)   indication whether some form of reply is required.

The actual layout of the form can vary; but a typical example is shown in Fig. 4.2. The format is usually more elaborate in a large dealership or group, where more people will be involved.

BUSINESS LETTERS. Most books on business communications lay down exact conventions for the layout and format of different types of business letter. Generally speaking in recent years the approach to business letters has been relaxed and many conventions have been less rigidly applied; the general trend is for letters to be more personal. Typical layouts for such letters are shown in Fig. 4.3(a) and (b). These examples show, the sender's address (usually pre-printed); the address of the recipient; a reference code for filing; and a main subject heading (for other than very short letters). The salutation is usually 'Dear Sir'; or in the cases where people have met or are in regular contact, the

BELVEDERE GARAGES GROUP

Ref. DS/EW

Motor Department Manager
The Majestic Insurance Group,
20 The Square,
Wembly,
Middlesex.

Dear Sir,

Ref. Hillman Hunter CBJ   797N

May we confirm the total cost of repairs to be £185.50, as agreed with your engineer Mr. Moore on 15th July, 1976.

Yours faithfully,

D. Sanders. T. Eng. (CEI) M.I.M.I.
Service Manager

Fig. 4.3(a)

BELVEDERE GARAGES GROUP

Our Ref.   CWG/LK   Your Ref.

Mr. F. Dowson,
6 Cleveland Close,
YORK YK3 P9S

Dear Sir,

    I acknowledge receipt of your letter in answer to our recent advertisement for a General Manager to be responsible for one of our large dealerships, and would confirm that we will contact you in due course if we wish you to attend an interview.

    For your further information I would advise you that the successful applicant will be based at our Manchester or Liverpool branch, and will be directly responsible to the Chief Executive for the efficient and profitable running of the dealership.

    In the meantime I would appreciate your completing the enclosed application form and returning it to me as soon as possible.

Yours faithfully,

D. Curry

D. Curry.

Chief Executive.   BELVEDERE GARAGES.

Fig. 4.3(b)

---

sender can refer to the recipient as 'Dear Mr. ——————'. The main text of the letter should be courteous and written in plain English using short sentences; and should avoid too many stereotyped phrases such as 'with reference to' or 'in reply to'. To close the letter use 'Yours faithfully' for a 'Dear Sir' letter, or 'Yours sincerely' for a 'Dear Mr.——————' letter. Avoid flowery phrases such as 'I am sir your obedient servant'. The sender's name and position in the dealership should be typed below the signature, since signatures themselves are often illegible.

The above types of communication involve the spoken or written word. A third type of communication, which indeed was one of the very earliest forms, is *visual communication*. Although developing from primitive origins this type of

communication has gone through a revolution during this century with developments in the mass media such as films and television, so that it now forms an
integral part of modern living. These and other more simple types of visual
media can be used in many applications in a dealership, which include the
following:

CHARTS

These fall into two categories; the familiar technical chart, which is usually
produced by manufacturers to show exploded views of complete vehicles or
units; and the business or statistical chart, which is used to present facts and
figures in a pictorial form. There are many varieties of such charts. The ones
more commonly used in the motor trade are:

Pictograms. Often pictograms are used to represent figures or technical data to
an audience which is not familiar with them. The figures are represented by
simple outline pictures. For example the number of mechanics employed in the
retail motor industry over a period of time could be represented by a shadow
outline of a person in an overall holding a spanner, each such symbol representing
100 mechanics. Likewise each 1000 cars sold over a given number of years could
be represented by the shadow outline of a car. This type of pictorial chart is
often used by the television news programmes to present statistical material.

Graphs. Graphs are based on two axes drawn to a scale. Values are then plotted
by marking comparative readings on both the horizontal and vertical axes. The
points plotted are then joined by a line; either by straight lines from point to
point or by drawing a smooth curve through the midst of the plotted points to
show a general trend.

Bar charts. These are a type of graph on which the heights of the bars are used
to represent numbers or values. Fig. 4.4 shows a bar chart prepared from
R.T.I.T.B. figures, showing the percentage of total manpower in the road transport industry against company size.

Gantt chart. This type of chart takes its name from the management pioneer
Henry Lawrence Gantt (see Chapter 1) who was the first to use it. It uses

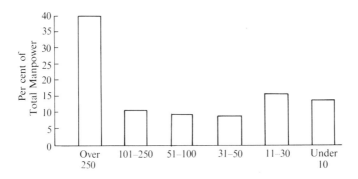

Fig. 4.4   Bar chart

horizontal bars to show planned performance, actual performance, and cumulative results. Fig. 4.5 shows a simple Gantt chart for the sales of a particular car over four budget periods. The width of each column represents eighty vehicles. The cumulative total is the sum of the bars in the actual sales line. This type of chart can be used in a more elaborate form, where the width of each column represents the planned figure for each period; the actual and cumulative figures are then drawn in as a fraction of that value. A simple form of Gantt chart similar to the one shown in Fig. 4.5 is used by many workshop control offices to check available time against time sold.

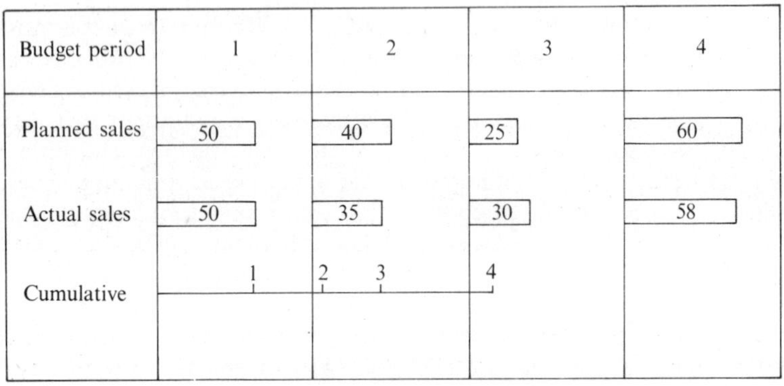

Budget period	1	2	3	4
Planned sales	50	40	25	60
Actual sales	50	35	30	58
Cumulative	1	2 3	4	

Fig. 4.5   Simple Gantt chart

Wall Posters. These can prove a very effective means of mass communication. If they are to give maximum impact they should be colourful and dramatic and put their message over simply. Many outside organizations publish excellent posters, particularly in the areas of health and safety. A forceful well-produced poster usually has little visual competition in most work areas, and will be effective for a certain period of time. If a poster remains on a wall for too long it becomes too familiar and loses its effect. To avoid this the poster should be removed after a short period and placed back on the wall at a later date if necessary. One large motor-trade group has successfully run a poster design competition for employees and the results have been very effective. When designing posters the following guidelines are useful:

> Messages should be clear and simple.
> Cover only one topic per poster.
> Use as few words as possible.
> Make the drawing simple and relevant.
> Gain maximum effect by using colour, humour, or dramatic effect.

FILMS AND SLIDES

This title covers a whole range of slides, still film-strips, and movie films or video equipment. This type of equipment has developed rapidly in recent years under the influence of educationalists and the various industrial training boards.

The many excellent films and film-strips produced by manufacturers of vehicles and components fall into either the marketing or technical categories. The main uses of these media in the retail motor trade are for training, advertising, and promotion. Films produced by outside organizations tend to contain too much irrelevant information. Slides, on the other hand, can be used selectively, only the slides required for a particular topic being used. A 'sound-track' can be provided by means of a long playing record or a tape cassette.

COMMITTEE PROCEDURE

Committees and meetings have been used more and more in recent years, to such an extent that meetings have come in for some harsh criticism on the grounds that they can be excessively time-consuming or can be used as an excuse for non-availability. If meetings are to be effective it is important that they do the job they are intended to do, and are not time-wasting. The difference between a meeting and a committee is not always clear, but in general it is accepted that a meeting is a group of people who meet to exchange or pass on information, or to make a decision. A committee usually makes collective decisions by a majority vote, and is responsible to a higher authority for its decisions and actions. The degree of formality can vary with the type of committee. Formality implies the following of an established procedure, in order to transact the business in an orderly and efficient manner. Nevertheless it is possible in a democratic committee meeting to waive parts of the formal procedure if all the members agree. For example minutes can be sent to members before the meeting and then taken as read, thus avoiding the standard procedure of the secretary reading them.

The Secretary. The secretary is responsible for all correspondence relating to the meeting and the arrangements for and recording of the meeting as it progresses, and therefore cannot be expected to be a full participant as well. The secretary is usually responsible for booking the office or room in which the meeting is to be held. He must then draw up the agenda, which is a numbered list of headings covering the business to be dealt with at the meeting, and is usually drawn up in consultation with the chairman. The heading of the agenda usually includes the date, time, and venue of the meeting. A typical agenda (which follows the standard pattern) is shown in Fig. 4.6. During the meeting the secretary must make notes in order that his minutes will be a true record of the meeting. The minutes have two main purposes: firstly to pass a record of the meeting on to the higher authority; and secondly to act as a 'memory jogger' to the members before the next meeting. The pace of the meeting at times can make it very difficult to record notes, but this need not be a problem since not all minutes require details of the discussion. The important item is the decision taken.

The Chairman is the leader of the meeting. The effectiveness of a committee depends to a large extent on the effectiveness of its chairman. The characteristics of a good chairman are that he has the personality to lead and control the meeting without forcing his own views on the members. He must at all times be impartial, even though he may disagree strongly with the decision being

---

SAFETY COMMITTEE

CHAIRMAN :   Mr. M.J. Maddison,   Secretary: Mr. A.D. Pengilly,
              Assistant Service Manager,   Works Office,
              Warwick Road Department.   Morden Road Department.

Dear Sir,

A meeting of the safety committee will be held in Office 3 at WARWICK ROAD Department on Wednesday 5th February, 1976. I hope you will be able to attend.

Yours faithfully,

A.D. Pengilly

AGENDA.

1. Apologies for absence
2. Minutes of meeting held on November 1st, 1975
3. Matters arising from minutes
4. Correspondence
5. Report of H.M. Factory Inspector to Central Department
6. Report by safety officer on implementation of Safety and Health at Work Act for each department
7. Accident involving R. Bolton at Warwick Road Depot on January 20th, 1976
8. Any other business
9. Date and venue of next meeting

Fig. 4.6   Agenda for a committee meeting

taken (this can prove very difficult at times!) The chairman's main duties are to:
ensure that the meeting is properly constituted and operated in accordance with the rules;
see that the meeting is conducted correctly, order is maintained, and irrelevant discussion is avoided;
ensure 'fair play' for all members;
judge the appropriate time for taking a vote, and see that the correct procedure is observed;
sense the general feeling of the meeting and sum up when no official vote has been taken;
make sure that the secretary has a true record of the proceedings;
send information through the secretary to the people who will have to implement the committee's decision, or who will be affected by them.

Committee Members. The effectiveness of a committee depends on the active participation of all members. In order to participate fully a member must do some preparation before the meeting. The object of circulating the agenda before the meeting is to allow members to prepare for it by collecting information, facts, and ideas, and making brief notes to ensure that they make positive contributions to the proceedings. If each member does this, meetings will be much more meaningful and effective, and less time-consuming.

PRESS CONTACTS.

Most dealerships which handle new and used cars advertise regularly in the local press and so have an established contact with them. Occasionally a small garage or a larger group will be in a situation where they gain prestige and good publicity (bad publicity is easily come by). When the occasion arises it can be advantageous to draft a report oneself and send it to the newspaper office. Alternatively, if the occasion warrants it (for example at the opening of new premises) the press can be invited to attend to cover the event. It is important that they should be given the correct facts and figures, and the best way to ensure this is to prepare handouts for them and to arrange for a responsible person to escort them. This can help to avoid a situation where reporters have to 'glean' information from unreliable sources.

QUESTIONS

1.   Discuss the importance of communications in the day-to-day running of a medium-sized garage. Clearly identify two different forms of communication and indicate where it would be appropriate to use each.   (I.M.I.)
2.   The trade press frequently publishes articles which influence the operation of a service repair department. Comment upon any recent article you have read and draft a short memorandum to your manager suggesting how the contents may be applied to your organization.
                                                                   (C. & G.)
3.   Vehicle manufacturers regularly send out service information which usually goes to the service manager. Some items are of such a nature that certain members of Sales and Spares Departments should know of them. How would you ensure that not only the members of the service department but also those concerned in the other two departments know of them?   (I.M.I.)
4.   Some writers hold that communication is the essential problem of management. Explain why communication is a problem, and state some of the methods which can be used to deal with it.   (I.M.I.)
5.   Various members of the management team have complained from time to time: 'Nobody tells me anything'. What are the main barriers to communication? As general manager what steps could you take to secure effective communications within your organization?   (M.A.A./I.M.I.)

CHAPTER 5

PERSONNEL

'The important thing to me is to get value for money'.

This statement could well be made by the all-important customer who requires the service offered by the garage; it could equally well be made by the garage manager as he reviews his labour costs. The common factor in each case is the *employee*. The customer or the manager can only achieve a high degree of satisfaction if a loyal, interested, competent, and highly-motivated staff are placed at all levels in the dealership.

The personnel function has to be carried out in any organization, irrespective of its size. The ideal situation is to have a Personnel Manager or Personnel Department, but this can only be justified in the minority of large motor-trade groups and road-transport organizations. In the vast majority of motor-trade establishments the personnel function is carried out by line managers (with the assistance of the general office), and it will be assumed for the purpose of this text that this is the case.

An enlightened manager will be aware of how much money is invested in his staff. This is clearly illustrated if he calculates the ratio between investment in equipment in a department and the money expended in wages in the same period. This will show that employees are a manager's greatest asset, and that he must make the best use of his human resources.

PERSONNEL POLICY

The policy of a business in relation to its employees should be clear and precise, and yet be applicable to all levels of staff. Like all policies, a personnel policy is best committed to paper. A general policy is shown in Fig. 5.1. This should be used as a guideline for supervisors and managers. Recent Acts of Parliament, in particular the Employment Protection Act (1975), increase the burden of personnel management resting on all employers of full-time staff. This Act gives employees and trade unions new rights, and erodes many rights that employers have traditionally held. The limited rights of the employer are explicitly laid down; and it is vitally important that managers and supervisors have a comprehensive knowledge of the Act, since failure to comply with its requirements can place an employer in a serious legal position. The most hazardous area of the Act refers to dismissal. No employee can be dismissed except in cases of 'grave misconduct connected with the business', and employees who consider they have been unfairly dismissed have the right to take their case to an

---

THE WHEATLAND MOTOR GROUP

Personnel Policy.

To offer regular and secure employment, with wages and salaries comparable with other dealerships in the region, with recommended rates of pay as a minimum. Financial and non-financial incentives applicable to the type of post will be applied by agreement between the management and the works committee.

Management will consult departmental representatives on matters affecting them, and workers' suggestions will be given due consideration in making management decisions. There will be facilities for each employee to discuss grievances, in the first instance with his supervisor and then with his departmental manager.

All vacant posts will be advertised, but promotions of existing staff based on experience and merit will be encouraged.

In cases of disciplinary action, verbal reprimands will normally be used, but severe reprimands will be given in writing by the manager of the department concerned.

A. Cairns.

General Manager.

Fig. 5.1

industrial tribunal, where the onus of proof of fair dismissal rests with the employer. It is therefore important that managers are fully conversant with all aspects of the Act, or, if in doubt, seek specialist advice from their Trade Association or Professional Institute, or from the Advisory Conciliation and Arbitration Service (A.C.A.S.), since any error can prove very costly.

MANPOWER PLANNING. A General Manager has two alternatives in dealing with his manpower requirements. He can either forecast and plan ahead, or wait until vacancies are imminent and then seek staff from 'what is available at the time'. The latter approach is only acceptable in small organizations, where labour turnover and numbers of employees required for expansion are small. A dynamic dealership will forecast the volume of business expected in each department, and from this develop a manpower plan covering requirements for non-skilled and skilled workers, as well as clerical, financial, supervisory, and management staff. A short-term plan covering four or five years will cover expansion requirements (or reductions if necessary), with provision being made for further customer services, retirements, wastage, and supervisory and managerial succession. Long-term planning is more difficult and less accurate, and is dependent on the volume of sales and service, the national economic situation, the financial strength of the company, and current government policies. With so many intangibles only an outline plan can be developed; but this is preferable to no plan at all.

No matter how small the garage, the manager should be aware of his approximate staff requirements for at least four years ahead.

SOURCES OF RECRUITMENT. Having drawn up a manpower plan, a manager must carefully consider different sources for the recruitment of staff, depending on the type of post vacant and the personnel budget. Available sources include the following:

Secondary schools and technical colleges. These can prove a useful source of apprentices and trainees for all types of work. It is a definite advantage if the manager has personal contact with careers masters, youth employment officers, and technical liason officers. The image of the dealership can be improved and recruitment of the most suitable young people ensured by co-operating with the schools to provide short terms of work experience for selected pupils; and by participating in careers conventions and careers evenings, where representatives of the dealership can meet prospective young employees and their parents.

Skills centres. These offer a free service in most towns, and handle vacancies for skilled workers and clerical staff as well as for supervisors and managers.

Recommendations from existing staff. If a reliable member of staff with a good record is willing to sponsor a new employee it is reasonable to expect that he too will be reliable.

Notices on the forecourt. A public notice in a prominent position is an inexpensive method of 'broadcasting' current vacancies to the present staff, customers, and the general public. If used consistently it can help to avoid needless enquiries, which can be time-wasting.

Local television. Many local I.T.V. stations, as well as commercial radio, offer some form of 'situations vacant' service on a local or regional basis. (This service is organized by the Department of Employment.)

Advertising in the press. A good advertisement is one that will attract a small number of applicants of the right type and with the necessary experience and qualifications. The format and information in an advertisement are all-important and are best left to a professional; an example is shown in Fig. 5.2. The range of publications in which vacant situations can be placed is quite varied and includes:

Local Newspapers	
National newspapers	— e.g. the *Daily Telegraph* and the *Guardian*
Trade journals	— e.g. *Commercial Motor, Motor Transport, Autocar, Motor Trader*, etc.
Journals of Professional Institutes	— e.g. *Motor Management* (I.M.I.) and *Road Transport Engineer* (I.R.T.E.)

JOB DESCRIPTIONS. If a manager is to be able to select the most suitable person for a particular job he must be familiar with the requirements of the job.

LONDON BRICK COMPANY LIMITED
&
MARSTON VALLEY BRICK COMPANY LIMITED

are altering the structure of their Group's Transport
Department and now wish to appoint

TWO AREA TRANSPORT SUPERINTENDENTS

The Group	operates a fleet of over 900 vehicles from a number of Depots.
The Job	Each Superintendent will be responsible for an area operating approximately 200 vehicles.
The Locations	One will be in the Peterborough area and the other in the Bletchley/Buckingham area. The Superintendent will be expected to live in the area for which he is responsible.
The Men	appointed will have a thorough knowledge of Road Transport Legislation, be experienced in Management and Industrial Relations. Their expertise will be mainly on the traffic side and they will be capable of supervising the daily routine and routing of the fleet.
The Rewards	will interest men earning £1,500 or more at present, and include provision of a Company car, non-contributory pension scheme and profit-sharing bonus.

Fig. 5.2   A recruitment advertisement in 1973

In a small garage the manager will be familiar with all the jobs, often from personal experience. In a large dealership the range of jobs is more varied and line managers are more remote from the work situation of each job. If a man is to be 'matched' to a job it is important that an accurate profile of each job is available, the profile's degree of sophistication depending on the type of job. The job description form is usually a pre-printed form and can include such headings as:

Job title	Location in dealership,
Summary of job content,	Training required,
Experience necessary,	Physical and mental effort required,
Responsibilities,	Working conditions.

Examples of job-description forms are shown in Fig. 5.3. These show a standard format. In a smaller garage they could be reduced to handwritten notes or summarized as a checklist to be used at the interview.

JOB SPECIFICATIONS. A job specification describes the human and personal qualities which are necessary to perform the job adequately. They include such headings as education, training, experience, initiative, physical qualities. Some confusion has arisen over the use of the terms 'job description' and 'job specification'. This is because in practice the two are often combined and

WHEATLAND MOTOR CO. LTD.

JOB DESCRIPTION

TITLE: Service Bay Operator   *Department:* Service.
          Semi-Skilled

GENERAL PURPOSE: Routine lubrication and maintenance of vehicles,
                               including inspection of components.

DUTIES: Lubrication and servicing of cars and light commercial
                               vehicles in accordance with manufacturers' schedules.
                               General lubrication.
                               Changing and checking of oil and fluid levels.
                               Visual inspection of chassis, suspension, steering and
                               braking systems.
                               Acting as assistant to the service-bay technician.

RESPONSIBILITIES: Recording servicing carried out on pre-printed record
                               forms.
                               Ensuring that each vehicle leaves the service bay in a
                               clean and roadworthy condition.
                               Recording stocks of oil, fluid, etc., weekly.
                               Directly responsible to the service-bay technician
                               for carrying out these duties.

JOB REQUIREMENTS:
Training: Experience in routine maintenance and servicing work,
                               knowledge of manufacturers' schedules.

Qualifications: As above.

Mental and
Physical Effort: Must be physically fit.
                               Must be observant through the working day.
                               Must be aware of the vehicle-safety and customer-
                               satisfaction aspects of the job.

JOB CONDITIONS.
Working Conditions: To work in a centrally-heated, tiled service bay fitted
                               with automatic recoil dispensing equipment, using a
                               'wheel free' vehicle hoist.
                               Facilities for washing and changing overalls adjacent
                               to the service bay.

Special hazards: Hazards associated with high pressure compressed air
                               and greasing equipment.
                               Lifting vehicles on hoist.

                               Evaluated by E.R. Gibson.

                               Date   4:4:76.

Notes.

Fig. 5.3   Job description

classified as a job description, which would be more correctly entitled a 'job analysis'.

APPLICATION FORMS. These are usually used for skilled jobs and supervisory and managerial posts. An application form is a standard form on which an applicant is asked to fill in his or her career and personal details in sequence. The areas covered usually include:

personal details:	family, home background
general education, examinations:	school career with examination successes
further education:	examination successes related to the post
previous employment:	past career in chronological order
hobbies and interests:	related and unrelated to the motor trade
references and testimonials:	from responsible persons and past employers.

An example for application for an apprenticeship is shown in Fig. 5.4.

INTERVIEWING. It will be assumed for the purpose of this paragraph that the interview is being conducted by the manager alone. In practice, for supervisory and managerial posts, the interview would usually be carried out by a panel representing general management and the department involved.

An interview is used almost universally for selection, and is a face-to-face encounter in which the interviewer endeavours to assess each candidate. The basic aim is to match an applicant (described on the application form) to the job (described on the job description). A systematic approach to an interview begins before interview day in that some pre-planning is necessary.
The manager must ensure that:

the number of candidates is known,

the distance candidates will be travelling is known,

arrangements have been made for reception of the candidates,

a suitable room is available,

adequate time is available.

The room or office used should be warm, light, and free from interruptions (including telephone interruptions). There are two distinct approaches to an interview; the pre-structured formal approach, and the unstructured informal approach. The most effective is a balance between the two, encouraging a relaxed atmosphere which puts both interviewer and interviewee at their ease, yet still retaining a basic structure such as the National Institute of Industrial Psychology (N.I.I.P.) Seven-Point Plan. This plan was developed by Professor Alex Roger and used by the Institute in vocational guidance projects. The plan is based on the seven basic attributes of:

Physique	Interests
General intelligence	Circumstances
Special aptitudes	Disposition.
Attainments	

THE DALEHOLME GROUP (MOTORS) LTD.

Gerard Street,
Newcastle-upon-Tyne

APPLICATION FOR APPRENTICESHIP

Please use block capitals.

SURNAME _____ FORENAMES _____

DATE OF BIRTH _____ NATIONALITY _____

Enter in the space provided details of full time education at school or college.

School or College	Form or Class Code	Dates of Attendance

Enter details of any examinations you have passed or failed in the past two years (or are about to take).

Examining Body.	Year.	Subjects	Level	Results

List any positions of responsibility held at school (e.g. prefect, group leader, captain).

List any formal organization of which you are a member, with positions held. (e.g. Scouts/Guides, Youth Club)

Have you a good health record? _____

Have you any physical disability?
If so, state its nature. _____

If offered an apprenticeship are you willing to undergo a medical examination by the group G.P.?

Date _____

SIGNATURE _____

SIGNATURE OF PARENT/GUARDIAN _____

Fig. 5.4   Application form

Item	Attribute	Essential	Desirable	Contra-Indications
1	Physique	Normal health Good vision Below 16 years 3 months.	15 yrs. 6 months	History of persistent illness
2	General Intelligence	Average C+. Above 50th. Percentile	65th Percentile	
3	Special Aptitudes	Mechanical ability above average	Numerical ability Manual dexterity Spatial Ability	
4	Attainments	Good record in Secondary Technical or Sec. Modern School	Grammar School Education or 'A' stream Sec. Modern or Technical	Below 'B' stream Secondary Technical or Modern School
5	Interests	Practical constructive hobbies	Model builder Knowledge of cycles, cars.	
6	Circumstances	Home encouraging study	Background of craftsmanship	Over emphasis on financial return
7	Disposition	Persistence Willingness to invest time and trouble without *immediate* return		Inability to get on with people

Fig. 5.5(a) N.I.I.P. seven-point plan

Item	ATTRIBUTE	Well Above Average	Above Average	AVERAGE	Below Average	Well Below Average
1	Physique					
2	General Intelligence					
3	Special Aptitudes					
4	Attainments					
5	Interests					
6	Circumstances					
7	Disposition					

Fig. 5.5(b) N.I.I.P. seven-point score sheet.

The example shown in Fig. 5.5.(a) is applicable to a young person taking up training in motor engineering. It lists qualities which are essential to carry out the job, qualities which although not essential are desirable, and qualities which would be a definite disadvantage to the candidate. As each candidate is interviewed a simple mark sheet such as that shown in Fig. 5.5(b) could be used.

Warm Up. A relatively short period of time should be spent putting the candidate at ease. Initial 'interview nerves' can be overcome by informal questions, and tensions can be relieved by reference to a hobby or interest, knowledge of a particular make of motor car or group of companies, or the usual standby of football or sport. This helps to establish a friendly but business-like relationship.

Factual check. The interviewer will ask indirect questions relating to the candidate's personal, academic, and job history. This gives the candidate an opportunity to confirm and expand on information found on the application form. It also allows the interviewee to answer any queries the interviewer may have regarding the information on the form, e.g. the reason for a gap in dates given in chronological order.

Assessment. In the final stage the interviewer must try to assess the personal qualities of the candidate. This includes strengths and weaknesses in relation to the job, whether the candidate is the type of person to 'fit in' and work well with prospective colleagues, and personal qualities such as attitude to work, ambition, and drive. This is best done by using indirect questions so that the candidates must express their own thoughts and ideas.

At this stage the candidate should also be invited to ask questions about the job, and this, as well as answering the candidate's queries, also assists in the assessment of the individual's personal values.

In addition to the traditional interview other forms of assessment are used in some of the more forward-looking dealerships. Any method of assessment which cuts out guesswork and subjective results should be encouraged. These include different forms of intelligence, comprehension, problem-solving, or psychological tests.

Methods of selection for all types of motor-trade jobs have been developed in recent years, by some large trade groups, such as the Motor Agents Association, and also in particular by the Road Transport Industry Training Board, who offer a range of selection procedures, and job descriptions and advice on staffing requirements to 'inscope' companies.

INDUCTION. This is the process of introducing the newly-appointed employee to the dealership. The Contracts of Employment Act 1972 requires employers to provide the new employee with written conditions of employment. As well as complying with this Act is is desirable that new employees should clearly understand the conditions under which they are employed.

The induction process can be undertaken in a few minutes, a half day, or spread over a longer period of time if knowledge of a manufacturer's product is included as part of the scheme. This will depend on the range of services offered by the dealership, its size, and the amount of information the recruit will be expected to assimilate.

A typical induction scheme will include an introduction to:

the dealership or group and its policies,
names and locations of line managers,
the physical layout of buildings,
immediate subordinates and superiors,
how the department operates, and its relationships with other
     departments,
safety and health regulations,
welfare facilities,
personal services.
This information can be imparted in several different ways.

In a small garage a talk and a tour of the works with a manager or training officer can cover all aspects. In a large dealership the induction scheme may include illustrated lectures, tours of various departments, films, and manufacturers' courses.

However simple or however comprehensive the induction, it has been proved that a systematic scheme will help the new employee to become a fully effective member of the work-force more quickly and help to ensure job awareness and loyalty to the dealership.

LABOUR TURNOVER

This is the ratio of the number of employees leaving the dealership to the average number employed during a period of six months or a year. The figure is usually expressed as a percentage

$$\frac{\text{Number of employees leaving during the year}}{\text{Average number of employees during the year}} \times 100,$$

e.g. if the average number of employees at a dealership for 1978 is 50, and during that year 12 people leave

$$\frac{12}{50} \times 100 = 24 \text{ per cent.}$$

This gives a numerical value, but is not meaningful until it is compared with the turnover of similar types of motor-trade business in a given area or region. Comparisons could perhaps usefully be made at a regional M.A.A. meeting. Percentages are best compared at a regional level, since local factors outside the motor trade can effect turnover, for example, the general level of employment and attractions and fringe benefits offered by other industries (e.g. in development areas).

A more detailed analysis can be made if figures are calculated by departments, and take into account such factors as retirements, marriages, and dismissals.

The true value is important because it reflects the effectiveness of the dealership's personnel policy. A high turnover demands action, since it has a detrimental effect on morale, and on the image of the dealership; and the process of advertising, selection and placement can also prove to be an unnecessarily high overhead.

SAFETY AND HEALTH

This is the concern of everyone in the dealership, but as in other aspects of management the lead and example must come from the top. By employing people a manager assumes responsibility towards them. A worker in any particular position in the dealership reasonably expects that he will not be asked as part of his normal work to put himself in a position where he may be injured or his health endangered; or, if such dangers are present, that his manager will make these clear and take every possible precaution to minimize them. In recent years the motor manufacturing industries have seen a realization of the danger from the processing of lead and asbestos, and information gathered on this subject has been passed directly to the repair trade.

Certain aspects of safety and health at work are covered by government legislation such as the Factories Act 1961, the Offices, Shops and Railway Premises Act 1963, and the more recent Health and Safety at Work Act 1974.

Minimum observance of the law is not enough however: managers must ensure that general and specific safety objectives are attained; and a continuous review of safety requirements is vital, so that as working procedures change, parallel changes in safety measures are taken. Over-all production efficiency is directly improved if due attention is paid to health and safety, since absenteeism is reduced and the efficiency of all workers can be improved. A high accident rate indicates to a manager that an improvement in methods of supervision or working conditions is necessary. Important areas to be considered in motor-trade establishments are:

> handling highly inflammable liquids,
> the movement of vehicles,
> hoists and lifting equipment,
> the use of electric mains-operated tools and equipment,
> paint-spraying,
> vehicle-cleaning,
> dirty working conditions,
> the need for eye protection in welding and grinding.

Accidents do not occur by some abstract statistical law, or in ratio to the number of staff; they are caused usually by ignorance or neglect. It is vital that *all* employees should be safety-conscious and that awareness should be continuous and not just regarded as an element of training or of induction, to be covered and finished with. This can be achieved by using effective notices, wall posters, or safety bulletins; a large organization can justify having a Safety Officer.

WELFARE. This is rather difficult to define accurately, and includes the legal requirements such as heating, lighting, and sanitation as laid down in the Factories Acts. But it also includes such items as:

Canteen facilities. These depend basically on the total number of employees, and can range from the provision of mess and rest rooms to full catering facilities which are often sub-contracted to an outside catering firm.

Social activities. These include sports facilities such as a darts team, or a football or cricket team, entertainments such as private discos, dinner dances, and party bookings at public entertainments.

Financial welfare. This is related to indirect cash benefits such as holiday schemes, saving schemes, and apprentices' merit awards. Such activities are becoming increasingly costly in these days of inflation, but activities can be made as nearly self-supporting as is practical, and the remaining costs subsidized by the dealership.

TRAINING

In its broadest sense this refers to the acquisition of knowledge and skill. Training is not limited to young people. Established adult personnel at all levels in a dealership often can and do benefit from some form of training; and this applies to supervisors and managers as well as craftsmen. On the installation of a new piece of equipment, the persons needed to operate it may require special training, but likewise if a manager is to maintain a high standard of performance he must be up-to-date with relevant management techniques and good business practices. The types of training to be found in a dealership may be classified under the following job groups:

craft/technical

commercial,

supervisory,

management.

Clearly, a wide range of training facilities must be provided if the industry's long-term survival is to be assured. All too often managers and personnel officers who seek potential apprentices concentrate on the sixteen-year-old school leaver. While these will continue to form the bulk of those recruited, dealerships could profitably look at other age groups, i.e. leavers at the age of eighteen with G.C.E. 'O' and 'A' level passes. While this group will be unlikely to 'earn their keep' initially, their broader educational background will often make them candidates for management posts in the future.

There is no reason why girls cannot be considered for craft skills training; not all will be content with clerical and commercial jobs. Mature adults who have followed a course of retraining at one of the government-sponsored Skills Centres, possibly through the Training Opportunities Scheme, should not be overlooked. It is appreciated that some problems will have to be faced, and that the basic skills provided by such centres will need to be supplemented with a knowledge of the company and its products; but an employer who ignores this source of skills may be turning his back on a useful supply of labour.

APPRENTICE TRAINING. The motor trade, like many others in industry, has centred its training on some form of apprenticeship. The Concise Oxford Dictionary defines an apprentice as, 'learner of a craft; bound to serve, and entitled to instruction from, his employer for a specified term'. In the past, and to a lesser extent today, apprenticeship training meant simply putting a lad with a skilled worker, in the hope that, by some form of industrial osmosis, the required skills would be obtained. This form of training has often been referred to as 'sitting by Nellie'. When an intelligent and receptive youngster was trained by a skilled worker who had the ability to instruct and the opportunity to cover a range of skills, job-effectiveness was often assured. Unfortunately, the quantity and mix of these, and other success ingredients was proving insufficient to meet the industry's needs, in spite of the valiant efforts made by trade associations, educationalists, and a national joint council.

Under the Industrial Training Act (1964) training boards were set up to improve the quantity and quality of training in industry. The Road Transport

Industry Training Board was formed in September 1966. Sectors within its scope include the retail motor trade, passenger transport, and road haulage. The Board defined its function as 'encouraging training, adequate in quantity and quality, of persons over compulsory school-leaving age for employment in any activity within the Road Transport Industry'. An early step was to define the training recommendations for the various occupations within each sector. Obviously a large proportion of the Board's work involves apprentice training. Recommendations were published which recognized six vehicle trades specialisms, following the pattern shown in Fig. 5.6. At that time directly relevant further education courses did not exist. For the first time mechanics were classified as light or heavy vehicle craftsmen. During 1968/69 various representatives from educational institutions and examining bodies, employers, and the training board together considered what new courses would be necessary to complement the industrial training and experience the student was to receive in industry. Some further-education courses were amended and a new series of courses on motor-vehicle craft studies was introduced. The current range of training manuals available is shown in Fig. 5.7, and part of the training syllabus for stage one general training is shown in Fig. 5.8. A log-book system is used to record completed sections of each individual apprentice's training and further education at each stage. On completion of training the log-book may be endorsed by the R.T.I.T.B. as a certificate of training, and becomes the property of the apprentice.

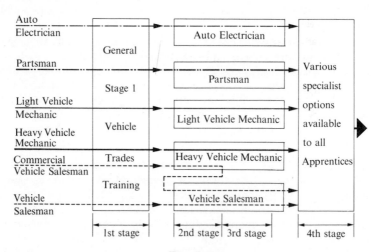

Fig. 5.6

TRAINING PROGRAMMES. The actual sequence of the training is flexible, and may vary according to local circumstances. Despite the efforts of the board and others to inform both employers and employees there still appears to be some confusion in the trade as to what is meant by education and training, and who is responsible for either or both. It must be clearly understood that industrial training together with properly planned and controlled experience is

---

TRAINING MANUALS

Vehicle Trades Apprentice Stage I

Vehicle Trades Apprentice Stage II
  Light Vehicle Mechanic
  Heavy Vehicle Mechanic
  Auto Electrician
  Partsman (Stage II, III and IV)
  Vehicle Salesman (Stages II and III)

Vehicle Trades Apprentice Stages III and IV
  Light Vehicle Mechanic
  Heavy Vehicle Mechanic
  Auto Electrician

Vehicle Body Trades Stage I

Goods Vehicle Drivers
  Carriage of Livestock by Road
  Drawbar Trailer Training
  International Driver Training
  Tanker Drivers Supplement
  Tipper Drivers Supplement

Public Service Vehicle Operatives
  Coach Driver Training

Driving School Instructors

Vehicle Sales Staff

Parts Marketing

Furniture Removals and Warehousing

Public Warehousing Operatives

Managers' Guide to Recruiting Warehouse Foremen

Agricultural Machinery Apprentices' Training Package
                          (+ VAT on £3.25)

On the Forecourt –
  Training Package

The Tutor's Guide –
  Training Package for Removals Estimators

Fig. 5.7   List of training manuals

the responsibility of the employer, helped and encouraged by the R.T.I.T.B. The purely educational element is catered for by the local education authority through colleges of further education, and is financed from public funds. Some of the more common types of training/education schemes are outlined below.

Day-release. In this system the education content is provided by a local technical college on a one day per week basis; the trainee being granted release from his place of work, with pay, for this purpose. The academic year runs from September to June. The industrial training is the responsibility of the employer.

AIM 6. ROUTINE VEHICLE SERVICE

Objective	Standard
a. The performance of typical functions concerned with routine vehicle servicing.	*a.* Ability to complete the following tasks efficiently and economically.

1. **Cooling Systems:**
   Draining, flushing, refilling, mixing of anti-freeze solution; replacement of radiator hoses.

2. **Lubricating Systems:**
   Topping-up, flushing, cleaning, oil and filter changes, identifying and selecting correct lubricants.

3. **Miscellaneous:**
   Tyre inflation, wheel changing, vehicle cleaning, e.g., washing and polishing of cars, steam cleaning of goods and passenger vehicle chassis etc. Replacement of simple components, e.g., sparking plugs, lamp bulbs and lenses, goods vehicle number plates and mud flaps.

Understanding of:—

Vehicle maintenance schedules.
The harmful effects that certain substances, e.g. brake fluid, have on coachwork, and the precautions to be observed.

NOTE: The following two aims should be satisfied where the Company has the appropriate departments, and where the apprentices are training for Parts or Sales work. For other categories this part of the syllabus may be curtailed or omitted.

AIM 7. SALES DEPARTMENT

Objective	Standard
a. Familiarisation with the Sales Department.	*a.* Understanding of the role and organisation of the Department. Understanding of the basic sales procedures within the Company.

AIM 8. ACCOUNTS DEPARTMENT

Objective	Standard
a. Familiarisation with the Accounts Department.	*a.* Understanding of the role and organisation of the Department.

Fig. 5.8   Part of a Stage One training syllabus

Block-release. In this system the trainee is released from work on full pay in order to attend a technical college on a full-time basis for a period of several weeks or months. The syllabus covered is the same as that of a day-release course. Similarly the industrial training aspect remains the employer's responsibility.

Integrated courses. These are courses of full-time instruction, covering both education and industrial training. The bulk of integrated courses are provided by technical colleges. This is an intensive form of training, and demands first-class facilities and conditions. The industrial training content of the course is charged to the employer and is fairly costly, but since facilities are available at colleges it is much more economical than the dealership setting up training facilities of its own. Work on the courses is continually monitored by R.T.I.T.B. staff. Approximately 50 per cent of Stage one apprentices train on integrated courses.

Group Training Schemes. These are used where a large motor-trade group or a number of independent dealerships in an area appoint a Training Officer to administer training programmes using the groups' premises, local colleges of further education, manufacturers' courses, and R.T.I.T.B. facilities. The system is most suited to more densely populated areas, and may involve up to as many as two dozen companies in a limited geographical area.

Group training centres. With this system a group of employers in a particular area form an association and, with assistance, both in staffing and finance from the R.T.I.T.B., set up a training centre to cover the industrial training requirements of the group. After the initial stages, finance is provided by a mixture of grant assistance and fees charged to the members. These groups usually form a close working relationship with the local college, which arranges the education course to run parallel with the training.

Technician training. The motor vehicle technician is in reality a non-existent creature. The technician can be readily identified in other industries, but in the motor trade 'technician' is a title that is used interchangeably with 'mechanic', or indicates a 'super mechanic' or diagnostician. Manufacturers, in particular Ford and British Leyland, have instituted postal product-training schemes, and Ford use the term 'technician'. The situation is further confused by the fact that a course is offered at most technical colleges leading to the award of the City and Guilds of London Institute Motor Vehicle Technician's Certificate. This course is only marginally linked with the R.T.I.T.B. training syllabus. The course content is more academically oriented than the craft studies series, and students embarking on the course have in the main better academic qualifications. A recently formed government-sponsored body is the Technician Education Council, which will set standards for technician education in all fields; and it is hoped to clarify the position in the motor-industry courses. Its formation opens possibilities of adding to the examination structure, and in the future this may well include certificates in supervisory or lower management studies.

Commercial training. This has often played the Cinderella in training, but the position is rapidly changing. The R.T.I.T.B. have published training recommendations for clerks. Office managers tailor their training to suit their own requirements, and commercial staff are generally encouraged to follow a course of study, usually on a day-release basis, in order to attain one of the recognized qualifications. The status of a secretary is usually based on office skills and the performance of the role of an aide. This implies a wider scope in education courses, taking in a range of topics such as economics, industrial relations, statistics, and management studies. Many colleges offer courses leading to the examinations of the London Chamber of Commerce and Royal Society of Arts in secretarial subjects. Other relevant courses of study in commercial subjects include Ordinary and Higher National Certificates in Business Studies; Ordinary and Higher National Diploma in Business Studies; and, for aspiring company

Title	Time	Content	Aids/Method	Given By
GENERAL: Invoicing 1. (a) Purposes of Department (b) Place in Organisation	20 mins.	Conversion of sales into revenue; price and cash flow controls; relationships to accounting process (etc.)	Job Descriptions Company Organisation Chart	Chief Accountant and Supervisor
2. Structure of Department	10 mins.	Nature of work; reasons for structure; allocations of duties; responsibilities of staff; level of demands of job and qualifications of staff (etc.)	Job Descriptions Department Organisation Chart	Supervisor
3. Operations	2 hrs.	Daily : Work note receipts Quality/accuracy controls Calculations of price rate Production of invoices Production of summaries Despatch (etc.) Weekly : Revenue statements Receipts controls (etc.) Monthly : Revenue statements Receipts controls Debt controls (etc.)	Documents A – Z	Supervisor Clerks 1 – 5
4. Methods Systems	1 hr.	Accounting Machines Standard Documentation Codes (etc.)	Machine Paper Flow Chart	Supervisor Machine Operator
5. Productivity and Controls	1 hr.	Minimum throughput standards Accuracy controls	Control Records	Supervisors
6. Input and Output	1 hr.	Link with: Operations Accounts Legal Customers	Flow Chart	Supervisor
7. Exercise	2 hrs.	*By Trainee* Statement of 5 restrictions or requirements imposed on other departments by invoicing and 5 imposed by other departments on invoicing; need for requirements, their effect on organisation, staffing and productivity.	Submit to Chief Accountant not later than .... Discuss with Chief Accountant and Supervisor within 2 weeks of submission.	

Fig. 5.9   One section of a management training syllabus

secretaries, the examinations of the Institute of Chartered Secretaries and Administrators.

SUPERVISORS AND MANAGEMENT. The professional bodies for establishing standards are the Institute of the Motor Industry, for the retail motor trade, and the Institute of Road Transport Engineers, for the road haulage industry. Details of both these bodies will be found in Chapter 7. Both Institutes are concerned with setting standards of performance and establishing ethical standards for managers in their respective industries.

Supervisors' training. Levels of supervision are not clearly defined in the motor trade or transport industry. The term supervisor can be defined as 'a person who through skills or ability is responsible for, and controls the work of others by close contact'. This implies management at grass-roots level, so that the supervisor is management's representative in the work-place, whereas management proper indicates a more remote type of responsibility and control. The lack of supervisory training in all industries has been acknowledged in recent years, and has led to the formation of the National Examination Board for Supervisory Studies (N.E.B.S.S.). Courses leading to the award of this nationally recognized certificate are available at many colleges of further education. The course involves a common core of work on supervisory principles and techniques, industrial relations, and financial topics, together with technical and legal aspects relevant to particular trades or industries. The schemes of work are flexible and directly related to local needs. Standards are continually monitored by N.E.B.S.S. representatives in order to maintain consistency throughout the country. Courses for supervisors in the p.s.v., road haulage, and retail motor trade sectors are offered in many areas.

Management training. The training board first published management training recommendations in 1969. These are based on a system of job descriptions and specifications which identify the purpose, scope, and responsibilities of the manager's job. These descriptions can then be linked to an appraisal of a manager's present performance and deficiences, and translated into training needs. In the larger dealerships or groups this leads to the development of a formal training arrangement which might include management-education courses, such as the Higher National Diploma with a Transport Studies bias, or the Diploma in Management Studies, also with a road transport bias. Various forms of short courses, seminars, and conferences are offered by colleges, manufacturers, professional institutes, management consultants, and trade organizations. When considering external course objectives, content and presentation should be carefully considered, together with the type of assessment and follow up. The courses, which are often quite expensive, must be relevant to, and form an integral part of the over-all training programme. To be effective the programme must be carefully constructed and documented. An extract of one section of a sample management training programme format is shown in Fig. 5.9.

To assist many small firms the Board adopted a rather unique approach when it established a specialist department dubbed T.A.S.C., 'Training Assistance in Small Companies'. The individual management training needs are catered for by specialist officers acting through a process of company visits and group training meetings. These arrangements allow for flexibility, and can be tailored to meet the specific needs of individual firms.

MANAGEMENT DEVELOPMENT.

This is an acknowledged concept to which, in the main, only lip-service is paid. In order to be effective any system of management development must gain its impetus from the practical involvement of the Chief Executive, who must set the tone. The firm's philosophy should permeate the chain of command. No manager or supervisor should be left in any doubt as to what is expected of him. Personal strengths and weaknesses will be identified and agreed corrective/development action implemented. Fig. 5.10 shows an example of one key task in a Sales Manager's job description and appraisal. A formalized approach to management development should greatly benefit both the individual employee and the dealership.

Key Task	Standard	Control
2.6. To ensure an increasing supply of business	2.6.1. When not fewer than x prospective new customers are canvassed each month	Sales Log: shows lowest monthly figure X + 20
	2.6.2. When not less than x per cent of quotations are accepted and result in a contract	Sales Log: shows percentage of successful quotations X — 5 per cent

Fig. 5.10   Example of one key task in a sales managers appraisal scheme

The Road Transport Industry Training Board, the Institute of Personnel Management, and others have carried out detailed studies of staff appraisal, job evaluation, job appraisal and job analysis, and have developed systematic methods of dealing with this type of work. The Institute of the Motor Industry and Institute of Road Transport Engineers have their own management syllabuses, which are, in many cases, closely linked to management training. These syllabuses are, however, intended to educate suitable personnel to a desirable professional level, and this book covers only a part of the over-all schemes.

QUESTIONS

1. Training should only be undertaken if it contributes directly to the achievement of the organization's objectives. Do you agree with this statement? Give reasons for your answers.   (I.M.I.)
2. What factors, both from inside and outside the organization, should be taken into account when preparing an estimate of the number and the skill categories of employees which a service repair workshop may require in five years time?   (C. & G.)
3. Given the job title of a supervisor state SIX tasks which might be found on his job description.   (C. & G.)
4. You have been asked by your manager to interview an applicant for the post of tester (cars) in your business. Set out in sequence the headings

of the notes you will use to conduct the interview as efficiently as possible.   (C. & G.)

Select a management post with which you are familiar (e.g. Service Manager) and state the main duties of the post.   (I.M.I.)

6. Briefly describe the personal qualities you would hope to find in the general manager of a large distributorship.   (M.A.A./I.M.I.)

7. Selection of personnel for a particular job is extremely important. State the requirements you would expect when appointing

      (a) An apprentice mechanic,

      (b) A skilled fitter,

      (c) A foreman,

      (d) A service manager.

8. If you had a vacancy for a management position in your company, describe the steps you would take to ensure it was filled in the most effective way.   (I.M.I.)

9. Industrial Training Boards emphasise the importance of Management Development. Explain what is meant by this term and why it is so important.   (I.M.I.)

10. As general manager how would you attempt to discover and develop the management potential of your staff so that possible successors to key posts may become available?   (M.A.A./I.M.I.)

11. The rate of loss of mechanics and technicians from your garage seems to be much higher than that of similar garages in your area. State possible reasons for this and suggest suitable action to reduce the loss.   (M.A.A./I.M.I.)

CHAPTER 6

HUMAN RELATIONS AND INDUSTRIAL PSYCHOLOGY

The term 'human relations' appears to have acquired several different shades of meaning, but on any interpretation the term can be applied perfectly well to the relations of people at work. The importance of the role of the individual in a large dealership is being recognized more and more, not only from the point of view of productivity but also as a major factor in building up morale. If a manager is to create and maintain an effective workforce he must be able to understand people; and for this reason all management training programmes should include at least the basic elements of industrial psychology. When asked if he would be attending a lecture on industrial psychology, the proprietor of a garage employing twenty people retorted, 'I know what makes my men tick, without fancy things like psychology'. His answer illustrates the common misconception that industrial psychology is not for down-to-earth people like garage managers; but in practical terms industrial psychology means precisely a knowledge of 'what makes people tick'. The gentleman quoted did in fact utilize industrial psychology at a practical level, which led to very good industrial relations in his small organization.

INDIVIDUALS AND GROUPS

In order to study human behaviour at work we will first study individual workers, each with his own pattern of behaviour, and then workers in groups, since any organization is made up of a number of groups.

INDIVIDUALS. The most obvious difference between individuals is in their appearance; but much more important to both supervisors and managers is the fact that each individual has his own pattern of behaviour, and will react differently to a given set of circumstances.

INDIVIDUAL NEEDS. Each worker has certain basic needs which can be likened in some respects to the basic instincts of wild animals, in that they require no teaching or learning and lie dormant in the subconscious until outside events bring them suddenly into the conscious mind, when they may cause the person concerned to act in a certain way.

Personality. This can be described as a pattern of behavioural dispositions, unique to the individual. Both heredity and the experience of the individual play a part in establishing this pattern. A person's attitude to his work, his personal values, interests, and actions all reflect his personality.

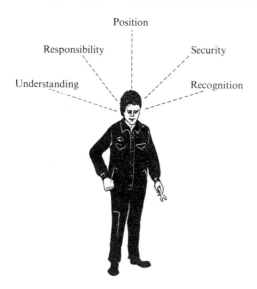

Fig. 6.1   Individual needs

Position. The desire for status makes an individual worker want to hold a certain position in relation to others. Sadly this need has often been overlooked in the motor trade and has been a contributing factor to high labour turnover. This type of drive is best illustrated by competitive sportsmen and political figures, but is found to a lesser degree in people at all levels in any organization.

Security. It is important to most workers at any level in a dealership that they can be reasonably sure that their job is secure for a given time-span, provided that they perform their duties to a reasonable standard. Details of job security should form part of a comprehensive contract of employment. From a purely financial point of view, if a dealership has recruited and trained a good reliable worker it makes good sense to retain him by offering him security.

Recognition. Each person working in an organization needs to be recognized as an individual and should never feel he is 'just a number on the pay-roll'. In a small garage this presents no problems, but it becomes progressively more difficult as the number of staff increases. As expansion and mergers take place it is important that individuals are not 'lost' in the larger organization. This can be best ensured by careful organization of the manager's 'chain of command' and the arrangements for supervision, so that the worker will never feel out of touch, and will gain direct praise and encouragement.

Responsibility. Individual workers are more likely to give of their best if some kind of responsibility forms part of their job. A special responsibility can make a worker feel that his job is important. When a manager delegates responsibility for a certain task he reduces his own work-load and at the same time adds to the self-esteem of the person to whom he delegates. The practice of making workers responsible for certain areas of work should begin at an early stage in their training, and can be a great motivating force.

Understanding. Each worker has a basic need to have his attitudes and the reasons for his actions understood. It is most frustrating for a person, at any level in an organization, if his superior continually turns a deaf ear to his point of view. An effective manager is one who is willing to do his utmost to understand his subordinate's point of view. This is particularly relevant when dealing with disciplinary matters, and is doubly important when dealing with younger employees and trainees.

The above items are more or less directly controlled by a manager, and when he is dealing with people he must continually bear them in mind. If these basic needs are not satisfied to some degree by the worker's over-all experience of his job, frustration occurs and may be expressed by the individual in several different ways.

Aggression. Most adults manifest their aggression in a non-physical way. Possible examples of this are the frustrated workshop foreman who has violent fits of temper, the typist who starts rumours about certain of her colleagues or the partsman who makes his workmate the scapegoat for a difficult customer (who is in fact the real cause of his aggression).

Fixation. This is usually revealed by a worker's repeatedly taking a course of action which he is fully aware will not achieve a satisfactory result. An example of this is a mechanic who insists on doing a particular job by a method which he knows from experience is inefficient and time-consuming.

Avoidance. Some workers habitually try to avoid certain work-situations, and either actually avoid them by swapping jobs with their workmates, or, if they cannot avoid doing the job, take no interest in it and tend to day-dream about outside interests.

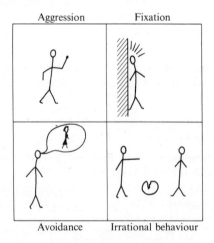

Fig. 6.2   Symptoms of frustration

Irrational Behaviour. This is a form of defence, and occurs when a worker acts in an irrational manner and then attributes the cause of his behaviour to one of his workmates. Occasionally a person who displays this type of defence-mechanism in an acute form will believe that his false statements are true.

These are four of the basic defence-mechanisms which counteract frustration, and which managers and supervisors should recognize as symptoms. The same symptoms may be produced by factors outside the working environment, such as personal, family, or medical problems. These cases are none the less the concern of the manager, since they will affect the person's performance at work. A manager must at all times be aware that there are reasons for every kind of human behaviour, and if he is to guide and direct his workforce effectively he must wherever possible discover the causes of any disturbed behaviour and deal with the situation in a helpful and constructive way. This is in the best interests of both the worker and the dealership.

WORKING GROUPS.

How does belonging to a group affect an individual? We can take the example of Mr. Newman who is taking up the post of technician in a large service-department workshop. On his first day at work the existing staff may be rather wary of Mr. Newman, who at this stage will be an isolated individual with his own attitudes, his own view of the job and the dealership, and his own methods of working. As time passes the barriers are broken down and Mr. Newman is accepted as a member of the group. The effect on Mr. Newman of becoming a group member is that he acquires a sense of belonging and security. His thoughts and actions will be affected by collective pressures within the group. This will to a greater or lesser extent change his attitude to his job, and he will tend to think along similar lines to the group. He will now also have a responsibility to the group as well as to his employer. The degree of change in Mr. Newman will depend on his individual make-up and on the strength and structure of the group. A perceptive manager will accept groups and appreciate that they go some way towards meeting the workers' basic need for security, recognition, responsibility, and understanding. His main objective must be to integrate the goals of the groups, under his leadership, with the goals of the dealership as a whole.

TYPES OF GROUP. Over the years management writers have sought to classify and name various types of group found in a working environment, but for the purposes of this book we will only consider the following classifications.

Primary groups. These are small groups of workers numbering from three to twenty who work together in a limited physical area, and who continually see and communicate with each other while they work.

Secondary groups. These are larger working groups consisting of people who do not have such a close working relationship. A secondary group is made up of a number of primary groups. An office with ten employees working together constitutes a primary group, while a service department employing seventy people would form a secondary group.

Informal groups. These are groups formed by people, often from different levels in the organization, which emerge naturally because of a simple need for friendship, or because of an area of common interest which may be connected with work or may be recreational, such as a pools syndicate or the rest-room dartboard. Groups of this type can prove a real challenge to the manager's authority if their activities are contrary to official authority; but can also be a great benefit, in that they may meet some individual requirements that official groups do not. This is particularly the case where the workers are involved in a repetitive type of work. One particularly important informal group is that of a group of workers who pass information unofficially. It is usually referred to as 'the grapevine' and is dealt with in more detail in Chapter 4.

In many respects an analogy can be drawn between a working team and a football team. Thus:

(i)   They both have a common purpose which gives the group a dynamic drive, and forms them into a highly motivated group. The group will attempt to achieve objectives either set externally by management or set and agreed upon by the group.

(ii)   A working group will be much more effective if the group leader (i.e. foreman or supervisor) is accepted by the group. The importance of this fact is illustrated by the detrimental effect on a football team of a captain who is not accepted by the players.

(iii)   They may have a past record of good work, high output, or objectives achieved. Each member then gains personal satisfaction because he can identify with success. This in turn leads to expectations of higher success, which will have the effect of knitting the team together and will help during periods of difficulty when the group's performance is below standard. The reverse also applies. If objectives are not achieved the group fragments, resulting in low morale.

The arrangement of groups is important from an output point of view, as well as from a human relations standpoint. Workers who are members of a highly motivated team will maintain a high output and find increased job satisfaction.

DISCIPLINE. Whenever a group of people work together to achieve a common purpose each individual tends to ignore his individual wants and urges and abides by a code of behaviour or set of rules which ensures the well-being and future of the group. There are two basic approaches to discipline.

Negative discipline. This is the type of discipline which is enforced, with workers having no voice in the formulation of rules, and not given any explanation of why the rules have been made. In practice this means that employees are led only through fear of punishment for violating rules. This type of discipline has a bad effect on morale and employee loyalty and its main failing is that workers tend to aim for levels of job performance and behaviour that will just avoid punishment.

Owing to social changes in the past few decades this type of discipline is no longer acceptable in the motor trade or any other industry. These changes include relatively high employment and even, in some cases, a shortage of skilled personnel. Better educational opportunities have led people to be more questioning in their approach to management and management decisions. This together with the increased activity of the Trade Unions, in particular over the past fifteen to twenty years, and legislation such as the Industrial Relations Act and the Trade Union and Labour Relations Act have led to the almost universal adoption of some form of positive approach to discipline.

Positive discipline. In this approach, rather than ruling by using penalties and fear, the manager's task is to develop a sense of responsibility in his employees so that discipline is accepted and self-imposed. The manager must still make use of his authority to make decisions where necessary, but employees should be involved in the decision-making process. This will ensure that, in general, decisions are acceptable; and penalties then assume a minor role, acting only as a back-up to standards that are accepted and understood by the working group.

INCENTIVES.

These can be defined as any scheme which encourages increased productivity. Incentives used in the motor trade can be classified as financial or non-financial, the latter being any incentive which is not a direct monetary payment.

FINANCIAL INCENTIVES. The basic methods of wage payment are as follows.

Time-based. This is where the worker is paid by the hour. It is used by a number of dealerships, particularly where the quality of work takes precedence over quantity. With this type of payment the supervisory and control system must ensure that the amount of time spent on jobs is realistic, so that payment is at least loosely linked with production. This type of control is often rigidly applied to the service department, but other departments such as the office and the parts department are less strictly controlled.

Bonus schemes. These are schemes by which extra cash is earned by increasing productivity. They are usually based on some form of target, the extra payment being related to the time saved. Two basic forms of bonus scheme on which others are based are the following:

(i)   *The Halsey Scheme*, in which the time saved is split on a 50/50 basis between the employer and employee.

If a job with a target time of 6 hours is completed by a mechanic in 4 hours then

> time saved is $6 - 4 = 2$ hours,
> bonus payed is $\frac{1}{2}$ of $2 = 1$ hour,
> total pay $4 + 1 = 5$ hours.

This scheme gives a limited incentive, since from the worker's point of view the more time he saves the more his employer gains. In order to counteract this impression other schemes have been devised where the proportion paid to the employee increases with the time saved. One typical such scheme is:

(ii)   *The Rowan Scheme*, where the amount of bonus earned is directly proportional to the time saved, i.e. the more time saved the larger the proportion paid to the employee. It is calculated from the formula

$$\frac{A}{T}\,(T - A)\qquad \text{Where } A = \text{actual time}, T = \text{target time},$$

e.g. If the mechanic again does the 6-hour job in 4 hours then under this scheme he would receive

$$\tfrac{4}{6}\,(6-4)$$
$$\tfrac{2}{3}\times 2 = 1\tfrac{1}{3}.$$

Therefore hour paid total 5 hours 20 minutes.

Advantages of bonus schemes

increased productivity, benefiting both employer and employee;
development of improved methods of working;
no need for close supervision — employees tend to be self-supervising;
provision of a direct incentive and a feeling of responsibility.

Disadvantages of bonus schemes

Quality of work may suffer unless adequate quality-control is exercised. Difficulties occur in agreeing realistic target times — those supplied by manufacturers are often modified in the light of experience.

Complex schemes can increase clerical and record work to the point where the effect of increased productivity is annulled by the increased overheads. The scheme can be difficult to operate effectively and fairly if the flow is intermittent or cannot be measured accurately.

Workers tend to be suspicious of a scheme they do not fully understand.

A scheme which overcomes some of these disadvantages and is in use in several large service departments is outlined below and in Fig. 6.3. The scheme relies on all charge-out rates being fixed before the scheme is put into operation. The mechanic or technician is paid a fixed percentage of the charge-out rate, regardless of the time taken. The amount of clerical work is minimized by using a modified three- or four-part job-card set, one of which is the customer's invoice.

Example using a four-part job-card set:

1. Reception office enters full details of the work to be done; and prices the labour at the full charge-out rate.
2. Two copies go to the service department office and two to the cost office.
3. The technician receives his job-card copy, which shows him what has to be done and the payment he will receive.
4. Parts are booked on the parts department copy.
5. While the job is in progress it is subjected to random checks by the quality-control supervisor.
6. When the job is completed and found to be satisfactory, the job card is signed by the tester.
7. The technician makes out a 'pay claim chit' for his percentage of the charge-out rate.
8. The job-card and 'pay claim chit' are passed to the cost office, and details of the technician's payment are entered on a weekly bonus chart.
9. The cost office check the job-card against their copy and complete the customer's invoice for parts and labour.

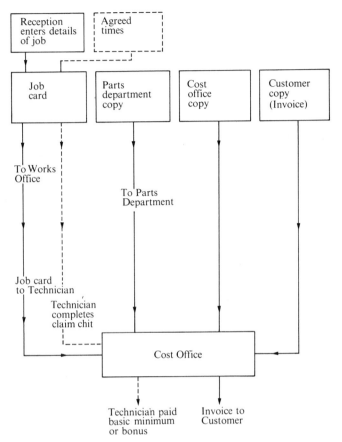

Fig. 6.3   Details of bonus scheme using a four-part job-card set

10.   At the end of the pay period the technician's earnings are totalled and
       checked against his guaranteed weekly earnings, and he is paid which-
       ever is the greater.
Some factors which must form an integral part of the scheme are:
a sound system of quality control;
agreement on overtime or bonus-only payment;
agreement on the payment of supervisors, testers and reception staff;
payment for work in progress but not completed (such as insurance repairs)
at the end of the pay period.
This gives the outline of a basic scheme which can be modified to meet local
requirements or the needs of a particular dealership or department.

MOTIVATION.

Consideration was given in Chapter 1 to the four basic management functions.
There is little question that the most enveloping of these functions is the
motivation of employees. The responsibility for motivation rests directly with

top management, since workers in a dealership will only be encouraged to give of their best if there is definite evidence of 'leadership from the top' which permeates down through the organization. If this lead is not given, the results in the long term are disharmony, discontent, and the development of a negative attitude. It is essential that a manager has a basic understanding of the motives which inspire men to work well. The importance of money is often over-emphasized when motivation is under discussion, and it has been proved that there are many other facets of job-satisfaction which are equally important in developing *esprit de corps*.

RESEARCH INTO MOTIVATION. One of the most widely accepted theories is that expounded by Professor A.H. Maslow, who identified a hierarchy of five basic needs, each of which develops successively as the previous one is satisfied. These are:

1. *Physiological.* This is the lowest level of human need, and includes the requirements for drink, food, shelter, and rest. All managers and employees view their work as fulfilling their needs at this level, by providing money to supply these requirements

2. *Safety needs.* When the physiological needs are satisfied a need for protection from hazards, dangers and the uncertainties of the future develops. These needs can be fulfilled to a large degree by safe working conditions, health and insurance schemes, and other fringe benefits.

3. *Social needs.* When the basic needs (1) and (2) above are largely satisfied higher-level needs naturally develop. The first of these is the need for workers to feel that they 'belong', and form part of the social group. Later studies than Maslow's have shown the powerful influence of group motivation, which can to a large degree help or hinder the manager or supervisor in achieving his objectives.

4. *Esteem needs.* These are closely linked with (3); they are the needs that people have for an individual sense of worth and importance. These needs are very strong, and it is often difficult to satisfy them in a typical garage organization with relatively few levels of authority. This presents a challenge to any effective manager, and still more directly to a supervisor. It can be met to some extent by a modern and realistic organizational structure, where workers with different skills can be grouped together; by a definite job rating system; by the conscious development of some form of career progression, which otherwise would often be lacking.

5. *Self-fulfilment.* Maslow sums up this need in his statement 'what a man can be, he must be'. If needs (1) − (4) are all satisfied an individual develops a sense of discontent if his potential abilities are not fully utilized in doing his job. Some jobs or methods of arranging jobs in the motor trade can lead to monotony. If this occurs the worker will look for fulfilment in other aspects of his working environment or outside work, both of which reduce his interest in the job itself.

An understanding of these basic needs will lead a manager to view his dealership's organization, working arrangement, careers structure, labour turnover, fringe benefits, and over-all performance as an indicator of how well these five basic needs are being met.

A second widely acclaimed theory is that arrived at after detailed research by Professor Douglas McGregor of the Massachusetts Institute of Technology. He observed that managers and supervisors adopted an approach to their work which reflected their own individual beliefs about their workers' needs and attitudes. In order to make comparisons he took the two most extreme points of view found in his research and referred to them as theory X and theory Y respectively.

Theory X is the traditional approach which developed during the Industrial Revolution and was strengthened by the Scientific Management Movement. In outline it states that:

(1) The average worker has an inherent dislike of work and will avoid work wherever possible.

(2) Because of this dislike of work, the average worker must be forced and coerced into carrying out his duties and threatened with punishment for non-fulfilment of duties.

(3) The average worker has little ambition, and prefers to be told what to do rather than to think for himself.

Theory Y has been developed during this century, and particularly since the 1930s, by Industrial Psychologists.

(1) Work can be a source of great satisfaction to an employee, given the right working environment.

(2) A worker is quite capable of exercising self-control and self-direction, and will strive towards accepted goals. This forms the basic philosophy behind 'management by objectives'.

(3) The average worker seeks responsibility, and is more stimulated by rewards and encouragement, both financial and non-financial, than by the negative approach of threats and punishments.

(4) The usual organization structures found in industry do not use to the full the capacities and potential of the majority of workers.

It is to be expected that very few motor-trade managers would be whole-heartedly theory-X-orientated, since this would reflect a negative attitude to their workpeople, the manager's most valuable asset. An effective manager will recognize that his approach will lie between these two extremes, depending on the calibre of his employees and the type of organizational structure. The general pattern that has emerged from modern research has shown that consistently high motivation is much more probable with an approach based on theory Y.

The future development of industry generally and the motor trade in particular will require that workpeople are highly motivated: both managers and supervisors will need to understand the intangible aspects of motivation, as well as the financial aspects. Leadership from management levels will become much less authoritarian; a more subtle and persuasive type of leadership will develop a sense of co-operation among all workers.

QUESTIONS

1. Explain what is meant by an 'autonomous work group' Why has this approach to running a business received so much attention recently?
(I.M.I.)

2. What is meant by the term 'motivation'? What aspects of motivation are of vital concern to the practising manager?   (I.M.I.)

3. Greater 'worker participation' is often quoted as the answer to industry's ills. Do you agree? Give reasons for your answer.   (I.M.I.)

4. Discuss the various ways in which managers may motivate their employees.   (C. & G.)

5. Why do people resist changes in working groups' methods and objectives? How can employee resistance to change be reduced?   (M.A.A./I.M.I.)

6. Give a brief summary of the facts of any one problem known to you arising from conflict or misunderstanding in human relationships in a garage business. State how you feel that the problem might have been resolved satisfactorily. Give reasons for your views.   (M.A.A./I.M.I.)

7. (a) State THREE types of incentive schemes suitable for operation within the service repair shop.

    (b) Explain in detail, the operation of ONE scheme.   (C. & G.)

8. What financial incentives and what non-financial incentives provide the best motivation for the service repair mechanic?   (C. & G.)

CHAPTER 7

MOTOR TRADE ORGANIZATIONS AND TRADE UNIONS

THE SOCIETY OF MOTOR MANUFACTURERS AND TRADERS (S.M.M.T.)

Established in 1902 for the primary purpose of representing the interests of the motor industry as a whole. The main objectives of the Society are to provide a means of formulating, communicating, and influencing the general policy of the motor industry with regard to industrial, economic, commercial, and technical topics; to encourage the efficiency of the industry by providing advice and information; and to develop the contribution made by the motor industry to the national economy. Membership is made up of four classes:

Honorary — used as a means of recognizing service to the motor industry by individuals.

Ordinary — being a British manufacturer of motor products whose sales amount to at least £200 000 per annum.

Associate — being engaged as a principal in a branch of the motor industry other than that of a distributor.

Retailer — being engaged in the distribution of motor vehicles.

Members are attached to one or more sections of the Society according to the nature of their business, with the members for each section voting for their representatives on the Council, which is the governing body of the Society, and consists of approximately one hundred members appointed annually. The organization of the committee structure is shown in Fig. 7.1, and that of the Technical Committees in Fig. 7.2. Details of the services offered to member companies are available from the various departments. The work of these departments is shown under the following departmental headings.

ECONOMICS. This provides information on motor industry forecasts and current economic trends in the U.K. and abroad.

EXHIBITION. This is responsible for organizing the International Motor Show and Commercial Motor Show and demonstrates a link with the original purpose of the Society, which was 'to protect motor manufacturers from exploitation by the organizers of motor car exhibitions'.

LEGAL. This advises members on legal matters. It scrutinizes pending government legislation and advises the Society on its implications, and advises members on individual problems.

COUNCIL AND COMMITTEE STRUCTURE

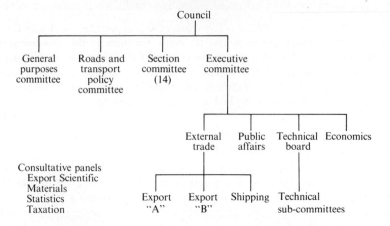

Fig. 7.1   Committee structure of the S.M.M.T.

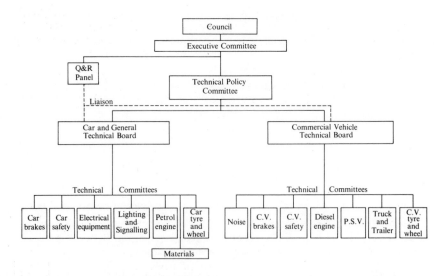

Fig. 7.2   Organization of the technical committees of the S.M.M.T.

TECHNICAL. This department is concerned with rationalization, standards for materials, and methods of testing. A major part of its work is involved with the technical aspects of national and international regulations affecting the design and construction of vehicles. This involves close liaison with the Government, the British Standards Institution, the Society of Automotive Engineers, and other international standards organizations.

OVERSEAS. This generally promotes the interests of the British motor industry abroad and keeps members informed of trading conditions in various countries.

PRESS AND PUBLIC AFFAIRS. The work of this department is closely linked with that of all other departments. Its main function is the dissemination, through the press, radio, and television, of news and of the views of the Society on matters affecting the industry. The Society has described itself as 'a forum for the motor industry', and exists to serve the interests of all member firms, large and small, both on an individual and on a collective basis.

THE MOTOR AGENTS ASSOCIATION (M.A.A.).

This is the major trade-association representing the retail motor industry in the United Kingdom (except for Scotland, which is covered by the Scottish Motor Trade Association), and has a membership approaching 20 000. It was founded in 1913. The Association is a democratic body controlled by a council elected from the membership and assisted by a number of specialist committees (Fig. 7.3). Administration 'in the field' is carried out by 17 Divisional Secretaries covering 21 divisions, such as Devon, West Midlands, North-East Counties, and Ulster. Each division is under the control of a divisional committee who meet regularly and act as a channel of communication between members and head-quarters. Membership is open to *bona-fide* motor traders who fulfil certain requirements relating to premises, staff, equipment, and ethical standards of trading.

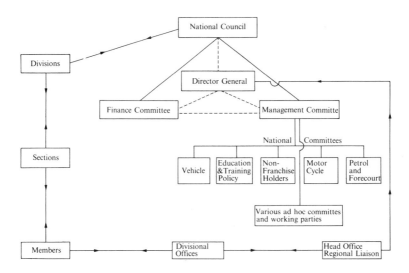

Fig. 7.3   How the M.A.A. functions

There are eight main grades of membership:

distributors, main dealers, and concessionaires,
retail dealers,
repairers,
three-wheeler, moped, and motor-cycle dealers,
petrol retailers,
auto-electrical engineers,
body repairers,
paint sprayers.

The services offered to members include the Association's magazine *Motor Trade Executive*, which reports on the trade generally. Advice can be sought on an individual basis on trading matters, legislation, wage agreements, legal problems, public relations, business stimulation, and profits; and there are also specialists recommended by the M.A.A. who can advise on such matters as finance, building design, and planning applications. In addition the M.A.A. organizes a national training programme for motor-trade apprentices; arranges seminars and short courses on topics directly connected with the trade; arranges reciprocal visits between the U.K. and overseas motor traders; and represents the employers on the National Joint Council. A role often overlooked is that the M.A.A. represents the retail motor trade at Government level, ensuring that an industry comprising numerous small units is represented by a forceful common voice.

Finally the M.A.A. administer an 'Investigation and Advisory Service'. The object of this service is to resolve disputes between members and their customers, in the first instance by informal conciliation and, if this fails, by arbitration by an independent professional arbitrator, whose decision is legally binding, thus avoiding court action. This scheme, along with the other activities of the M.A.A., goes a long way towards improving the image of the trade in the eyes of the general public.

THE NATIONAL JOINT COUNCIL FOR THE MOTOR RETAIL AND REPAIRING TRADE (N.J.C.)

This was established in 1943, and its work covers industrial relations in the broadest sense of the term. The council represents the interests of both employers and employees. It is composed, on the employers' side, of eleven M.A.A. members and one representative of the S.M.T.A., and on the employees' side of twelve members, representing the Transport and General Workers' Union, the Amalgamated Union of Engineering Workers, the General and Municipal Workers' Union, the Electrical, Electronic and Telecommunications Union, the Plumbing Trades' Union and the National Union of Sheet Metal Workers, Coppersmiths, Heating and Domestic Engineers. Their work covers wages and working conditions, conditions of employment, procedure to be followed in industrial disputes, and apprenticeship contracts. (A section of one of these contracts is shown in Fig. 7.4.)

Agreement of Apprenticeship in the occupation of. . . . .

made on the . . . . day of . . . . 19 . . . . , between:

THE EMPLOYER   . . . .

            of . . . .

            . . . .

THE GUARDIAN   . . . .

            of . . . .

            . . . .

THE APPRENTICE . . . .

            of . . . .

            . . . .

whose date of birth is . . . . .19 . . . . . .

IT IS AGREED

      1. That the period of the Agreement of Apprenticeship shall be . . . . years

. . . . months from the . . . . day of . . . . 19 . . . . .

      2. That the signatories undertake to observe and fulfil the several conditions and obligations set out in the Agreement.

      3. That if the period of the Agreement of Apprenticeship mentioned in Clause 1 is less than the normal period of apprenticeship prescribed by the 'Notes on Completion' printed on the first page of this form, any shorter period takes account of:

(a)   Continuance by the Apprentice in full-time education or approved training

appropriate to the occupation until . . . . 19 . . . . .

      or

(b)   The period from . . . . 19 . . . . . . to . . . . 19 . . . . . .

      spent in the service of another Employer which has contributed to the appropriate training of the Apprentice.

	The Employer	The Guardian	The Apprentice
(Signature)	. . . .	. . . .	. . . .
	In the presence of	In the presence of	In the presence of
(Signature)	. . . .	. . . .	. . . .
	(Witness)	(Witness)	(Witness)
(Address of Witness)	. . . .	. . . .	. . . .
	. . . .	. . . .	. . . .
	Occupation	Occupation	Occupation . . . .
	. . . .	. . . .	. . . .
	Date	Date	Date . . . .

Fig. 7.4   Part of apprenticeship agreement published by the N.J.C.

THE ROAD TRANSPORT INDUSTRY TRAINING BOARD (R.T.I.T.B.)

The Industrial Training Act (1964) made provision for improving the quality and quantity of training in British industries, and gave the then Minister of Labour (now the Secretary of State for Employment) the power to set up Industrial Training Boards. The R.T.I.T.B. was formed in 1966 and became the sixteenth Training Board to come into operation. The Board has twenty-eight members, consisting of a chairman, ten employers and ten trade-union representatives, and seven educationalists. The committee structure of the Board is shown in Fig. 7.5. There are two committees directly responsible to the main Board, namely the Finance and General Purposes Committee and the Training Policy Committee. Sub-committees dealing with specific aspects of the Board's work may also be established. Local administration is carried out by twenty geographically-dispersed area offices. In line with one aim of the Industrial Training Act, viz. 'to share the cost of training more equitably', the Board operates a levy/grant scheme. The Board collects money from establishments within its scope and liable to pay the levy, and awards training payments (grants) to firms carrying out training to standards determined by the Board. This basic scheme has been modified over the years, and at present consists of a rather complicated arrangement, whereby under certain circumstances, establishments which meet certain specified requirements can apply for exemption from the levy. Employers who do not apply for exemption can claim specific training grants. In addition to grants financed out of the levy, publicly funded 'key grants' are also available for certain kinds of approved training situations, among which may be recognized integrated apprentice training and off-job training centres.

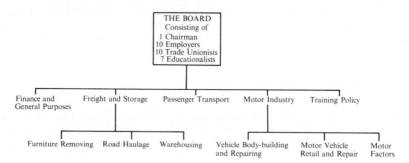

Fig. 7.5   The committee structure of the R.T.I.T.B.

Scope of the Board

The Board covers all aspects of road transport and allied sectors, including road haulage, passenger transport, all branches of motor vehicle distribution and repair, motor factors, and agricultural equipment repairers. Training recommendations cover many skills within these industries and include managers, clerks, craft apprentices, drivers, and salesmen.

Facilities provided by the Board

Training Assistance in Small Companies (T.A.S.C.). This is a unique service offered to small firms, in which training-board specialists determine the management training needs and arrange to cover these needs by off-the-job training phased over a period of time, plus an on-the-job advisory service. This minimizes the problems of staff being absent for long periods, and gives training tailored to the firm's individual requirements.

Multi-Occupational Training and Education Centres (M.O.T.E.C.). There are two M.O.T.E.C.s, one at High Ercall (near Shrewsbury) and the other at Livingston (near Edinburgh). Both provide first-class facilities for both practical and theoretical training, to supplement facilities in the industry and at colleges of further education. In the main, courses offered are of short duration – one to ten days – although apprentice training is an exception.

(c) *Group training schemes.* These are set up by a number of small- to medium-sized firms operating in the same geographical area. By joining together in this way they are able to avail themselves of expensive training resources which they could not afford individually. The facilities – staff, plant, vehicles – provide for their common needs. There are about 140 such groups.

(d) *Mobile training units.* These are mostly based on articulated vehicles, and provide an education/training area 13m by $2\frac{1}{2}$m. This type of unit can provide training on specific topics where facilities are not otherwise available.

(e) *Field training officers.* The Board maintains Training Officer staff 'in the field'. Among other duties they act as training advisers to employers, offer assistance to training centres and further education establishments offering integrated courses, and generally monitor the standard of training being given. Details of some types of R.T.I.T.B. training schemes can be found in Chapter 5.

THE INSTITUTE OF THE MOTOR INDUSTRY

The Institute was founded in 1920 and became 'Incorporated' in 1927. Its 'Purposes', as a Professional Institute, are a summary of the 'Objects' of the Institute's Memorandum of Association, and are now included within the regulations governing membership of the Institute under Article 6 of the Institute's Articles of Association.

The 'Purposes' are:
1. To set examinations which conform to the standards required for the award of qualifications for all levels of management within the motor industry.
2. To provide professional status to those employed in the motor industry by the granting of qualifications recognized by the motor industry and the public.
3. To increase members' knowledge of the industry.
4. To operate a code of conduct to enable the public and others within the industry to recognize and rely on the professional ethics of a member.

5.   To establish overseas branches and close links with organizations abroad whose activities are connected with the motor industry, with particular reference to Europe.

The Institute is governed by a Council of Management which appoints a number of standing committees.

Membership of the Institute is open to all men and women employed in the motor industry or in organizations connected with it. It is the individual who applies for membership, and not his firm, and election to membership depends upon the applicant's academic qualifications and/or experience and position.

The five classes of membership are:

$$
\text{Corporate Members} \begin{cases} \text{Fellow} \\ \text{Ordinary Member} \\ \text{Associate Member} \end{cases}
$$
Graduate
Student

(A registered Student of the Institute must be sixteen years of age or over, employed in the motor industry, and studying for the Institute's examinations.)

For administrative purposes the United Kingdom is divided geographically into Regions and Centres, which arrange their own lecture meetings and social functions. Some of these branches also have groups for Student and Graduate members. The Regions and Centres are administered by elected Committees of Corporate members, whose duties are to administer the Institute in their own area in accordance with the Articles of the Council of Management.

Among the services available to members are the Institute's Journal *Motor Management*, containing information about the Institute and articles of technical and managerial interest; a library, from which books may be borrowed free of charge by post or by personal application by members in the U.K. and Eire; an Appointments Register, whereby members are helped to find suitable appointments, and firms with a vacancy are encouraged to inform Institute headquarters when seeking qualified staff.

The Institute has a code of conduct under the authority granted to it under Article 6 of the Institute's Articles of Association. The code of conduct for members of the Institute, as set out below, was adopted for inclusion within the Institute's Regulations on 18 March, 1976.

The code of conduct is as follows:

MEMBERS WILL:
1.   Accept the code of conduct as a condition of membership of the Institute.
2.   At all times be strictly professional in their approach to the public, business colleagues, and all those whom they meet in their day-to-day business activities.
3.   Perform their duties and observe their responsibilities to their employers and staff and the public in a manner which shall in no way give rise to doubts of their integrity.
4.   Conduct their business with the dignity and skill expected of a professional person.
5.   Be proficient in the techniques of their business and employment.

6.   Keep abreast of developments, modern techniques, and Government legislation applicable to their employment, and take reasonable steps to ensure that the staff for whom they are responsible are kept fully informed of such developments.

7.   Take reasonable steps to ensure that work undertaken by their staff is performed in an efficient and honest manner.

8.   Give objective and reliable opinions when called upon to give professional advice.

9.   Encourage staff to raise their educational standards.

THE INSTITUTE OF ROAD TRANSPORT ENGINEERS (I.R.T.E.)

This is a professional institute which offers membership to persons employed in the road transport industry who are suitably qualified by age, industrial experience, and qualifications or exemptions from examinations. The grades of membership are Member, Associate Member, Associate, Graduate, and Student. Membership is considered by the Council after applicants have passed the necessary examinations and have made application for a grade of membership, giving details of practical achievements.

The main aim of the Institute is to improve the professional status of persons employed in the road transport industry by

(i)   improving the commercial, technical, and managerial skills and competence of persons employed in operating vehicles or transporting goods and passengers;

(ii)   encouraging developments in the design and construction of all types of transport vehicles to improve inspection, maintenance, and safe economic operation;

(iii)   encouraging the education and training of young people and offering recognized qualifications in order generally to improve their status;

(iv)   being involved in proposals for new legislation relating to road transport.

Local meetings are organized by local committees. Lectures are arranged on technical, managerial, and general topics allied to road transport. Most committees have at least one member (often a college lecturer) who is in a position to advise applicants on local college courses. Like the I.M.I., the Institute of Road Transport Engineers is controlled by an elected Council, and administration is carried out by a permanent staff at headquarters. A central library dealing in the main with transport engineering is available for members. The magazine *Transport Engineer* is published regularly by the Institute, and contains articles on management and vehicle operations, legal aspects and technical topics, (including comparisons of vehicle performance) as well as Institute news. In addition a monthly bulletin is published, which gives details of all forthcoming lectures and social events and current technical and legal information on news items. An annual conference, which consists of presentations of technical and managerial papers, together with an exhibition of vehicles and transport equipment, is well supported by members.

OTHER TRADE ORGANIZATIONS.

The principal organisations concerned with the retail motor industry have been mentioned. There are of course many organizations to cover the needs for each section of the industry. By careful scrutiny of trade papers in local libraries or college libraries it is possible to find references to these many associations. Managers should familiarize themselves with such associations and with trade papers, for such familiarity is necessary to keep their ideas up-to-date. Failure to do so could mean advantages for diligent competitors.

TRADE UNIONS.

There is a long tradition in Britain for workers in particular trades or crafts to form associations. Examples of these are to be found in the medieval guilds. These were made up of both employers and employees. Associations representing the workers alone first appeared as Friendly Societies or Workers' Clubs, but in the main these fulfilled a social function rather than dealing with conditions of employment. Trade Unions as we know them today came about with the Industrial Revolution. This very rapid transition from rural industries to capital-intensive industries employing large numbers of people and using more machinery led to a change in the environment of the workers. The skilled craftsman no longer had the expectation of progressing to become a master of his craft. The loyalty found in the old family firms no longer had a place, and workers tended to transfer this loyalty and allegiance to the newly-formed Trade Unions. These groups provided a means by which the workers could register their dissatisfaction with their working environment. The formation of Trade Unions was seen by the establishment as a definite threat, to the extent that the Combination Acts of 1799 and 1800 made grouping to form trade unions illegal. In the course of various repeals and reintroductions of similar Acts trade unionism developed through several distinct stages. The latter half of the nineteenth century saw the development of what was called 'new-model' unionism. These unions were made up from the ranks of highly skilled craftsmen in such industries as engineering, textiles, and mining, as well as those traditionally associated with the craft guilds. New-model unions developed for the first time a national structure with strong central control. One of the first of these unions was the Amalgamated Society of Engineers (1951), which was the forerunner of the Amalgamated Union of Engineering Workers which is currently active in the motor and transport industry.

It was also during this period that the legal standing of trade unions was enhanced and their efforts co-ordinated by the formation of the Trades Union Congress (T.U.C.) in 1868.

The development and extension of the new-model unions stimulated the thousands of unskilled workers then employed in the iron and steel, building, and service industries (such as the railways and the gas supply industry). These workers had a more militant attitude, and criticized new-model unions for their conservative attitudes and their policy of 'non-strike action wherever possible'. This stimulation led to the development of what was called 'new unionism'. The membership of 'new unionism' unions consisted of relatively poor unskilled workers, and as the early unions of this type became recognized, more were formed. As their strength increased they endeavoured over a period of time to gain parliamentary representation, and several union members stood as 'working class' candidates, but gained little support. The trade unions needed represen-tation in Parliament in order to change the Master of Servants Act, which placed severe restrictions on working people; and also to secure legal safeguards for the increasing union funds. In 1900 the T.U.C. set up a Labour Representation Committee to assist trade unions in bringing pressure to bear on M.P.s to improve the law relating to trade unions and to introduce improved industrial and social legislation. This committee became the Labour Party in 1909, and most unions broke their ties with other political parties and became affiliated to the Labour Party.

During the industrial boom and period of high employment which followed the First World War the unions amassed large funds, and their financial strength seemed secure beyond doubt. But by 1921 more than fourteen-and-a-half million workers were either out of work or on strike, and the funds of many unions, including the Amalgamated Union of Engineers, were exhausted. Increasing unemployment and demands from employers to reduce wages, led to lay-offs, lock-outs, and increasing tensions between the government and employers, on the one hand, and the trade unions and the T.U.C. on the other. The General Strike was called on 19 May, 1926. It was to prove damaging both to industry and to the trade unions. The impact of this strike did not reach its full potential, because non-unionized workers and volunteers worked to maintain essential services. This was particularly the case in the road transport industry, where most drivers and mechanics carried on in conditions as near normal as possible. Many members saw the failure of the strike as a major blow to the trade unions; but with the exception of the miners most workers went back to work on the same conditions and rates of pay that existed before the strike. The great benefit that came out of the strike was that conciliation rather than conflict became an accepted aim. This great belief in conciliation was a favourite doctrine of such strike leaders as Ernest Bevin. A second result of this conflict was that the idea of a static basic wage was established; and from this time employers ceased to approach periods of financial difficulties with the view that wages could be slashed, and began to view wages as a standard business overhead.

Following the general strike, legislation was introduced to curtail the rights of trade unions and their members. This was the Trade Disputes and Trade Union Act (1927), which outlawed strikes, lock-outs, sympathetic strikes, and actions aimed at coercing the government or inflicting hardship on the community. This Act was completely repealed in 1946, when the Labour Party came to power after the Second World War. Recent major legislation affecting trade unions was the Industrial Relations Act (1971). This was a very comprehensive Act, its basic aim being to improve industrial relations in Great Britain. It consisted of seven main features:

1)   A code of practice covering industrial relations.
2)   Definite rights and protection for individuals.
3)   Definitions of unfair industrial practices, including infringement of an individual's rights to join or not to join a trade union.
4)   New methods of settling disputes, involving bargaining rights and the recognition of trade unions.
5)   Protection for the community at large during emergencies which threaten public safety or health.
6)   A system of judicial institutions and an extension of the scope of industrial tribunals.

7)   A system of registration for employer's' associations and trade unions, which ensured certain privileges and immunity from court action arising out of industrial disputes only to bodies that were registered.

Parts of the Act were unpopular with many trade unions, most refused to register under the Act, and some as a result suffered financial and legal penalties. The end result of this opposition was the Trade Union and Labour Relations Act (1974), which repealed the Industrial Relations Act but re-enacted, with some modifications, the parts of that Act relating to unfair dismissal and retained the code of practice. It lays down provisions relating to the status and regulations of trade unions and employers' associations; gives workers protection against exclusion from membership of a trade union, and rights to terminate membership; sets out new definitions of a trade dispute; and gives certain legal immunities to those carrying out certain acts in connection with picketing, against breaches of contracts of employment, and against actions against a trade union for tort.

Structure of trade unions

Approximately half the working population in Britian are members of a trade union or staff association. The general trend since the Second World War has been towards the formation of larger unions as a result of amalgamations. This pattern has followed closely the pattern of change in industry, with the number of employees being drastically reduced in the coal-mining and textile industries, and a rapid expansion in the fields of transport and service industries. Also during this time more and more 'white-collar' workers have become organized. The two main trade unions active in the motor-trade and road-transport industries are the Amalgamated Union of Engineering Workers and the Transport and General Workers Union. The A.U.E.W. membership is drawn in the main from workers with engineering skills, and the union is termed a craft union, while the T.G.W.U. is a large union covering a wide spectrum of skills and occupations, and attracts members from many large road-haulage and public service vehicle operators. This type of union is often referred to as a general union, and the T.G.W.U. is the largest trade union in Britain. Various unions are represented on the National Joint Council for the Motor Vehicle Retail and Repairing Trade; the employers are represented by the Motor Agents' Association. A typical trade-union structure consists of local branches (having direct contact where necessary with the executive council) and representatives on District, Regional, and National Committees. These in turn have representation on the Executive Council, which in a general union is made up of representatives of regions or territories and from the constituent trade groups.

The Trades Union Congress (T.U.C.)

This forms the hub of the British trade union movement, and consists of member unions which are voluntarily affiliated to it. The T.U.C. is the main policy-formulating body of the trade union movement, yet, unlike its counterparts in some other countries, it has no direct disciplinary control, but gains its strength and influence from the fact that more than 90 per cent of all trade-union members belong to unions or associations affiliated to it. The everyday running of the T.U.C. is in the hands of a permanent headquarters staff headed by the General Secretary, whose appointment is approved by Congress and who remains in office until he or she retires. Congress meets annually, with delegates representing each affiliated union. The main work of the Congress is

(i)   to elect the thirty-five-member General Council,

(ii)   to discuss the annual report.

A card system of voting is used at Congress. This gives representation according to the number of members in any particular union: a representative is allotted one card vote for every 1000 members.

Function of trade unions

In broad terms the function of a trade union is to ensure security of employment wherever possible; to gain improvements in working conditions, wages and the standard of living of workers; and to raise their status and vocational opportunities.

The shop steward

He or she is the representative of the trade union in the workplace. Unfortunately, owing to the stress laid upon certain unrepresentative incidents by the media the shop steward has become a stereotyped character, who, though seen by the workers as a person to take their troubles to, is seen by the manager as the person who is going to bring him trouble.

The shop steward's true vocation lies at neither of these poles. He or she must look after the interests of the members as outlined above, but must also communicate with management and follow agreed procedures for dealing with problems and disputes. It is of the utmost importance that managers appreciate the function of shop stewards and develop a co-operative relationship with them; this can lead to great improvements in industrial relations. Unfortunately personalities are directly involved in this relationship, which can prove a real problem. Since shop stewards are more and more likely to be educated and trained for the job, the manager must avail himself of similar background work if an effective management/trade union relationship is to develop. This relationship can be turned to positive advantage, in that a steward with close and detailed personal knowledge of the workers and their conditions can resolve grievances within a small group, and decisions can be reached quickly. Although employees in some of the larger organizations in road transport and most of the large P.S.V. operators have been union members over a long period of time, there has been little union activity in the retail motor trade, the main reason for this being the fragmented nature of the industry, with approximately 80 per cent of companies having less than 10 employees. However in recent years unions have become more active in attracting members, particularly in the larger organizations. A manager cannot turn a blind eye to this development; he must be realistic and take a positive attitude, ensuring that the intervention of a trade union is a means of improving industrial relations rather than a head-on clash of employer and shop steward.

QUESTIONS

1.   As the Managing Director of a company in the retail motor trade, describe the policy you would adopt to meet the increase in Trade Union representation.   (I.M.I.)

2.   Outline the origins of the Trade Union movement in Great Britain. What are the principal functions of the unions today?
      What developments in trade unions are likely in the immediate future?
                                                                    (C. & G.)

3.   Explain the composition and function of the National Joint Council for the Motor Vehicle Retail and Repairing Trade.   (C. & G.)

4.   Explain the composition and function of the following motor trade organizations:
            The Society of Motor Manufacturers and Traders;
            The Motor Agents' Association;
            The Institute of the Motor Industry.

RECOMMENDED READING

Fundamentals of modern management by J.S. Dugdale (Brodie)
Management: its nature and significance by E.F.L. Brech (Pitman)
Organisation: the framework of management by E.F.L. Brech (Longman)
The practice of management by Peter F. Drucker (Heinemann)
Business administration: an introductory study by O.S. Hiner (Longman)
Industrial administration and management by J. Batty (Macdonald and Evans)
The reality of management by Rosemary Stewart (Heinemann)
Business administration and management by C.S. Deverell (Gee and co.)
Industrial administration by J.C. Denyer (Macdonald and Evans)
Principles and practice of supervision by R.J. Barnes (I.S.M.)
Supervisory studies by Peter Wilfred Betts (Macdonald and Evans)
Improving management performance by J.W. Humble (B.I.M.)
Management by objectives by G.S. Odiorne (Pitman)
The effective executive by Peter F. Druker (Heinemann)
Computers in business by N.C.C. (B.B.C. Publications)
Computers in business studies by Harold Lucas (Macdonald and Evans)
Business communications by R.T. Chappel and W.L. Reed (Macdonald and Evans)
The practice of industrial communication by Michael Ivens (Business Publications)
A textbook of business communications by R.T. Chappel and W.L. Reed (Macdonald and Evans)
The theory and practice of personnel management by M.W. Cuming (Heinemann)
Interviewing by J. Munro Frazer (Pitman)
Financial incentives by R.M. Currie (B.I.M.)
Industrial skills by W. Douglas Seymour (Pitman)
Principles of training by D.H. Holding (Pergamon)
The social psychology of industry by J.A.C. Brown (Pelican)
Industrial psychology by J. Munro Frazer (Pergamon)
Human aspects of management by G.W. Howells (I.S.M.)
Human relations in industry by Gardner and Moore (Irwin)
Trade unions and industrial relations by N. Robertson and J.L. Thomas (Business Books)

Much useful information can be gained from the publications of the various professional bodies such as:
The Institute of the Motor Industry
The Institute of Road Transport Engineers
The Institute of Personnel Management
The British Institute of Management
The Institute of Supervisory Management
The Road Transport Industry Training Board

The above list includes the I.M.I. recommended reading list with others selected by the author. It is important that students read widely on supervisory and management topics in order to increase their depth of management knowledge.

INDEX